SECRETS
of
THE VINE

BIBLE STUDY

For Personal or Group Use

LEADER'S EDITION

BRUCE WILKINSON
with DAVID KOPP

Multnomah® Publishers *Sisters, Oregon*

SECRETS OF THE VINE BIBLE STUDY LEADER'S EDITION
published by Multnomah Publishers, Inc.

© 2002 by Ovation Foundation, Inc.
ISBN-13: 978-1-590-52858-7

Cover design by David Carlson Design
Cover illustration by Katia Andreeva
Interior illustrations by John Lewis

Scripture is from *The Holy Bible,* New King James Version.
Copyright © 1982 by Thomas Nelson, Inc. Used by permission.

Multnomah is a trademark of Multnomah Publishers, Inc.,
and is registered in the U.S. Patent and Trademark Office.
The colophon is a trademark of Multnomah Publishers, Inc.

Printed in the United States of America

For information:
MULTNOMAH PUBLISHERS, INC.
POST OFFICE BOX 1720
SISTERS, OREGON 97759

04 05 06 07 146651086 08—10 9 8 7 6 5 4 3 2

DEAR BIBLE STUDY LEADER,

Welcome to the exciting and important ministry of leading men and women into a closer relationship with the Lord and into a more fruitful life for His kingdom. By taking up this challenge, you're deciding to pursue what mattered most to Jesus in His final conversations with His disciples.

On the night before He died, Jesus told His inner circle of friends, "I have called you friends, for all things that I heard from My Father I have made known to you. You did not choose Me, but I chose you and appointed you that you should go and bear fruit, and that your fruit should remain" (John 15:15–16).

You are called, chosen, and appointed for an awesome task: to make a difference in the lives of others, a difference that will count for all eternity. May God bless you abundantly for your willingness to be His servant and a blessing to others.

A PASSION FOR FRUITFULNESS

I wrote *Secrets of the Vine* to show how God works in our lives to bring us from barrenness to fruitfulness for His glory. The book is based on Jesus' teachings in a vineyard (found in John 15), where He used a memorable word picture to show how much abundance God wants from our lives, and how we can cooperate with Him to make it happen. If you haven't read this little book yet, I urge you to do so.

The study you're holding delves more deeply into what the Bible teaches about fruitfulness and shows in practical ways how each of us can bear fruit for God's glory.

More Christians than ever are realizing that spiritual abundance is not only possible but expected of every believer—and they don't want to settle for less. After reading *Secrets of the Vine*, a woman named Sarena jotted me a note: "I don't have another day to waste," she wrote. "I want to be a passionate Christian. I want to have an overflowing basket for God."

Whether you are a first-time group leader or a veteran teacher, you bring the same essential gifts to class:

◆ the truth of God's Word;
◆ a desire to serve God and help others;
◆ a complete dependence on God to do His work.

As you ask God to use these gifts each week, you'll hear inspiring stories from your students about what they're learning. You'll see lives change. And you'll change, too.

ESTABLISHING COMMON GROUND

To get your class on the same page, I strongly recommend that you lead the class in making three commitments:

1. Everyone agrees to read *Secrets of the Vine* or listen to the audio book at least once.
2. Everyone commits to spending one to two hours the week before class working through the week's material. Many students will want to do a couple of pages each day during their quiet time.
3. Everyone commits to asking God to change their lives to bring a greater harvest of fruit for God by the end of the class. After all, this isn't a study about just fruitfulness; it's an invitation to become more fruitful personally.

Another excellent way to enhance your study is to use the thirty-one-day *Secrets of the Vine Devotional* and the accompanying *Secrets of the Vine Journal* during the month of study. These learning tools will take you into a richer and more personal understanding of the material from John 15. Consider initiating a plan for the whole class to follow the devotional/journal as a parallel project during your four weeks of study.

For other related materials, see Recommended Resources in the general introduction of the Bible study.

STRUCTURE OF EACH SESSION

Each week, the study leads the class through a dynamic, life-changing process:
1. What do you really believe? (personal inventory).
2. Bible study on the main idea for the week (fruitfulness, discipline, pruning, abiding).
3. Deeper study on the biblical theme for the week.
4. Case studies of the key Bible characters that demonstrate the lesson.
5. Practical applications of the theme.
6. Confronting the major hindrances that are preventing life change, and changing your beliefs to conform to the truth.
7. Making a new commitment to live for greater fruitfulness.

HOW TO TEACH WELL

Prepare thoroughly for each session. Pray for each member by name. Ask God to first change you, then your class. Your confidence will increase dramatically as you become more familiar with the material. Use a New King James Version Bible if available (not required); this is the version on which this study is based.

Guide your class time with a firm but sensitive hand. You are not the answer person; you are the facilitator and encourager. Keep the discussion on topic and as close to your intended schedule as possible. Don't hesitate to direct the conversation away from dominating persons and pointless arguments. Everyone doesn't have to agree.

Share honestly from your own life, and invite others to do so as well. Talk about what you're learning, or still trying to learn, about the lesson. Keep the discussion focused on personal application, not abstractions.

The following icons highlight good starting points for lively discussions and will help you know how to order your class time for best results:

 indicates a key verse, definition, or explanation. Use this as a review tool and to make sure that you don't miss the main points.

 indicates optional material for further study. Use this icon to help you decide what materials you can leave for later. If you have limited time, it's better to do key parts well than to try to rush through all of it.

 *indicates a group process question that focuses on life experience rather than on the Bible text being addressed.*

W̌eek One

FRUITFULNESS

WHAT GOD WANTS FROM THE BRANCH OF YOUR LIFE

<u>Welcome.</u> Welcome your class to a study about how to live a fruitful and abundant life for God. The most important goals for this week are to help your students understand just how much God wants spiritual fruit from every Christian, and to motivate each class member to desire and pursue this in their own life.

Ask who has read the book *Secrets of the Vine* and what they thought about it. Invite people to share any personal learning goals for today's session on fruitfulness. These might be stated as questions or doubts they want answered.

<u>Getting Started.</u> Read aloud the introductory text and review the week's objectives listed in the "This Week You'll Discover…" box. Then open with prayer. Ask God to give every person in the class a greater understanding of the abundant harvest God has destined for them from eternity past.

 ### WHAT DO I BELIEVE ABOUT WHAT MY LIFE SHOULD "PRODUCE" FOR GOD?

<u>Question 1.</u> Ask for volunteers to share part or all of their answer to this question. Keep in mind that those students who don't feel they've accomplished much of eternal value may feel discouraged or even guilty. Assure the class that in the

coming weeks every one of them will discover exactly what God wants their lives to produce—and how they can cooperate with Him for greater results.

Question 2. Inventory. You'll find an inventory in the first section of each week of the Bible study. The inventories are intended to help provoke fresh thinking, not to define the problem or be comprehensive doctrinally. Keep this time fun. Ask your class to hold off on in-depth discussions at this point (a lot of questions will be answered as we go along). Invite your group to share inventory results—anyone surprised?

Talk Point. You might start by sharing your own response to this question.

2. WHAT IS GOD'S VINEYARD AND WHAT DOES IT MEAN FOR ME?

Questions 1–4. These questions are designed to give students a clear understanding of the word picture Jesus used in John 15. Ask your students if any of them have ever visited a vineyard and, if so, to describe what they saw. Make sure your class is clear on the difference between a branch and the vine. *[1.]* Jesus. *[2.]* Father. *[3.]* Christian or believer. *[4.]* Branch.

WHO'S IN THIS PICTURE?

This page is important for those students who are new or unlearned Christians. To process the page more quickly, assign the references to individuals and then go around the room and fill in the blanks together. Point out that although the Holy Spirit isn't mentioned in the vineyard picture, His role is critical in helping us to become fruitful. Jesus concluded His vineyard message with these words: "But when the Helper comes, whom I shall send to you from the Father, the Spirit of truth who proceeds from the Father, He will testify of Me. And you also will bear witness, because you have been with Me from the beginning" (John 15:26–27).

3. WHAT QUALIFIES AS FRUIT?

Question 1. You may want to emphasize the difference between the good works some mistakenly do to try to earn salvation and the good works that God calls us to do *after* we are saved. Talk with the class about why this distinction is so important. Key text: "For by grace you have been saved through faith, and that not of yourselves; it is the gift of God, not of works, lest anyone should boast" (Ephesians 2:8–9).

Question 3.

> ACTS 16:14–15—Hospitality.
> 2 CORINTHIANS 9:7–8—Giving.
> 2 TIMOTHY 4:5—Evangelism.
> JAMES 1:27—Caring for the needy.
> JAMES 5:14–15—Prayer ministries.

Question 4. Invite the class to share their answers.

Key Point. Remind the class that our motives for doing good works matter to God. You might reference Matthew 6:1–4. *What is a good motive?* For God to get glory; to help someone; to serve Christ, etc. *What is a wrong motive?* To earn glory for self; pride; to get something inappropriate in return, etc.

Question 5. Be sure to make the distinction that bearing fruit is something we *do*. If time permits, have the class list one outward good work that might spring from each one of the fruits of the Spirit listed.

Talk Point. If any students are still unclear about what "fruit" is, encourage the group to review the definitions and then discuss various scenarios that may or may not qualify as spiritual fruit and why this is so.

HOW IMPORTANT IS IT FOR ME TO BEAR FRUIT?

Question 1. Ask the class what special connotations the word *appointed* has. (For example, today people are often "appointed" to an office—given ultimate responsibility for accomplishing something important.)

Talk Point. [Question 1.] Steer the class away from feeling guilty about good works they haven't done and encourage them instead to let this question be motivating. From now on, they will want to watch more carefully for those opportunities to do the good works God planned for them. *[Question 2.]* In addition to their skills and talents, it might help the class to think in terms of people they are in a unique position to influence. If the class is familiar with *The Prayer of Jabez*, point out that every person who is part of our territory is also a prime candidate to be a recipient of our good works.

HOW MUCH FRUIT DOES GOD WANT OR EXPECT?

Question 1. Ask the class if they're surprised to learn that results and quantity matter greatly to God. Discuss how and why they may have thought differently until now.

Key Point. Remind the class that though God is most pleased with and glorified by the branch that bears "much fruit," His *love* for us is not based on what we produce. Rather, our love for Him should motivate us to be as fruitful as possible.

Question 2. When I ask this question of Christians around the world, audiences invariably conclude that 50 to 60 percent of believers produce "no fruit," about 35 percent produce "fruit" or "more fruit," and only 5 percent of Christians bear "much fruit." Discuss your class's observations; why do they think these numbers are true?

Question 3. Invite those who are comfortable doing so to share their answers and explain their conclusions. Reassure those who are having trouble quantifying their level of fruitfulness that as they work through the study the answer will become clearer.

WHAT CAN I LEARN FROM A BIBLE CHARACTER ABOUT FRUITFULNESS?

Question 4. Point out that though sin robs our ability to bear fruit, it never takes Christians permanently out of the running. God's goal is always restoration and greater abundance.

Question 5. There's a strong trend these days to measure our love for God by how strongly we *feel* love—for example, during a moving worship experience. Yet Jesus clearly links love for God with an *action* on our part—for example, obedience and good works. Ask the class how easy it is for them to separate their love for God from their willingness to do good works for Him. How might connecting the two help them to bear fruit?

Question 6.

> ACTS 2:38–41—Thousands respond to Gospel.
> ACTS 3:1–8—Healed lame man.
> ACTS 4:8–13—Could see they had been with Jesus.
> ACTS 5:14–16—Ministry of apostles.
> ACTS 10:34–48—Reaching out to the Gentiles for the first time.

WHAT CAN KEEP ME FROM A FRUITFUL LIFE?

Allow your class time to process their responses privately. Ask them to choose one or two of the attitudes or beliefs that are their greatest obstacles. Have them look up the corresponding references and write out their new breakthrough belief. Afterward, invite them to share comments or personal "ahas."

This is an important time to nail down new ways of thinking and commit to acting on them. Now that your group understands their new beliefs, they are ready to make a commitment.

MY NEW START IN A FRUITFUL LIFE

Pick someone from your class to read the text aloud, then give everyone time to write in the box at the bottom. Turn the page for your closing prayer. Suggest that the groups prays it together aloud.

In closing, ask your students how they're feeling about the Bible study: Are you moving too fast? Do they still have unanswered questions? How could class time be improved for next week? As a send-off, remind your students to look for opportunities to do good works during the coming week. Encourage them to spend time on next week's lesson.

Week Two

DISCIPLINE

HOW GOD MOVES YOU
FROM BARREN TO BOUNTIFUL

Welcome. Report on the week: "How has knowing that God's destiny for you is fruitfulness changed your thinking or actions in the past week?"

Getting Started. Read the introductory text aloud and review the week's objectives listed in the "This Week You'll Discover…" box. Then open with prayer. Ask God to give you willing hearts as you learn more about how He intervenes in your lives when your branch bears no fruit.

WHAT DO I BELIEVE ABOUT
GOD'S INVOLVEMENT IN MY LIFE?

Question 2. Inventory. Invite your group to share results. Explain that being fully convinced that God _does_ actively intervene in our lives is foundational to this week's teaching. Some class members may have always thought that our lives are ruled by circumstances and fate rather than any direct intervention on God's part. Assure those who scored low on the inventory that what they will learn in the pages ahead may surprise them but that the results will be both positive and life-changing.

Question 3. The prospect of God disciplining them may leave some of your students startled or fearful. Assure them that once they understand more about His methods and motives, they'll discover that God's loving intervention is actually very good news.

HOW DOES GOD RESPOND
WHEN MY LIFE IS UNPRODUCTIVE?

Question 1. Before you move on, you need to point out two extremely important truths from this verse. Ask the class to underline the two key phrases:

[1.] _"Every branch in Me…"_ Jesus was talking here only about believers. The New Testament repeatedly describes believers as being "in Christ" (2 Corinthians 5:17).

[2.] _"…that does not bear fruit."_ Sadly, it's possible to be "in Christ" yet produce no fruit for a time. Jesus wanted His followers to know that even though such a condition is possible for a Christian, it is never desirable.

Question 2. God's goal in discipline (besides bringing about a change in our behavior) is always one of loving restoration. He reaches down to rescue us and brings us back to Himself.

Question 3. After your students have answered this question privately, ask if they can now see a correlation between unfruitful times in their lives and ongoing sin in their lives.

Key Point. Your class may ask what the Bible means when it says, "If anyone does not abide in Me, he is cast out as a branch and is withered; and they gather them and throw them into the fire, and they are burned" (John 15:6). Christians through the ages have wrestled with Christ's application of vineyard terms like "takes away" (v. 2) and "throw them into the fire" (v. 6). For that reason we should allow for a range of understanding within the body of Christ. It's helpful, however, to note some key facts about this passage:

[1.] His subject is fruit-bearing, not personal salvation.

[2.] His audience is the eleven chosen disciples, those whom He describes as "in Me."

[3.] His teaching method is by visual analogy or similitude. In other words, Jesus is using a picture to make a comparison—in many ways, Christians are *like* grape branches. (We're not *exactly* like them or literally made of wood and leaves.)

In this context, Jesus makes a dramatic point to show that a branch that clings to sin can become worthless for its intended purpose.

Jesus makes a similar visual comparison in Matthew when He says, "You are the salt of the earth; but if the salt loses its flavor, how shall it be seasoned? It is then good for nothing but to be thrown out and trampled underfoot by men" (5:13). Does Jesus mean that ineffective Christians should literally be cast on the ground and walked on? Of course not. As with the fruitless branch, this comparison is drawn to make a point about unrealized potential. We should understand Jesus' teaching in the vineyard in the same way.

Respect your students' individual viewpoints in this discussion, and help them avoid getting into theological arguments. If someone interprets this Scripture to signify a potential loss of salvation, that doesn't lessen the importance of the vineyard truths we are focusing on in this study. In fact, it's all the more reason to heed Jesus' words.

UNDERSTANDING GOD'S MOTIVES IN DISCIPLINE

Question 1. Read the passage aloud to your class and then fill in the blanks together. Query them about how convinced they are about what these verses reveal about God's motives. Which of these scriptural truths surprise them, and why?

Question 2. You might help the class process this question by asking them what mistakes earthly parents commonly make. For example, reacting in anger rather than love; abusing physically or emotionally; over- or under-disciplining; failing to take action; and being inconsistent or unfair. Then point out that we can put the word *never* in front of each one of these to describe God's discipline.

Talk Point. Be prepared to hear from students who experienced abusive discipline at the hands of a parent or other adult. If you sense that this is a painful and deeply felt issue for someone, encourage him or her to pursue healing outside of the study. (Do they need to forgive? Do they need counseling?) Avoid letting the class get mired in one person's personal experience or story. Keep the focus on what we know to be true of God.

WHAT DOES GOD DO WHEN HE DISCIPLINES ME?

Level 1. *[c.]* Pastor. *Levels 1–3.* If time permits, ask the class to think of one example they have either experienced or witnessed for each level of discipline. Encourage those who are comfortable to share their answers. Discuss why they consider the incidents as rebuke, chastening, or scourging.

Key Point. Be sure to remind the class that we should never confuse God's discipline with His condemnation or punishment. Jesus paid the price for our sins (Colossians 1:13–14; 1 Peter 2:24). When the Father intervenes in our lives, He isn't trying to get us to *pay* for our sins but to *stop* them. The pain we experience in God's discipline is not meant for harm or retribution, but to bring us back into right relationship with Him and return us to the abundant life we were created for.

COMPARING THE LEVELS OF DISCIPLINE

Question 1. Take a minute or two to let the class study the chart and then briefly discuss answers to the question.

Question 2. If time permits, try this experiment. Ask the class what percentage of Christians they believe endure scourging. Ten percent? Thirty? Then take them back to Hebrews 12:6 and point out that He "scourges *every* son whom He receives." All Christians have been or will be severely disciplined by God. How does your class feel about this?

Question 3. Pause for a moment of silence while students contemplate and answer this very private question.

WHO ELSE IN THE BIBLE EXPERIENCED GOD'S DISCIPLINE?

ASA

Question 1. *[a.]* Verses 7–9: Rebuke—Hanani the seer verbally rebukes Asa. *[b.]* Verse 10: Chastening—it's apparent by his actions that Asa was now experiencing severe emotional distress as a result of his disobedience. *[c.]* Verse 12: Scourging—Asa's rebellion led eventually to debilitating illness and death.

Question 2. Point out that not every rebuke we receive is from God or related to spiritual discipline. Contrast when Jesus rebuked Peter (Mark 8:33) and when the disciples rebuked those bringing young children to Jesus (Matthew 19:13). Discuss ways in which we might determine whether a rebuke is actually from God.

JOSIAH

Question 1. Josiah received a rebuke by reading God's Word (the Book of the Law). For example, in Deuteronomy Josiah discovered the severe consequences (curses) that God said would come as a result of continuing disobedience (see Deuteronomy 28).

Question 2. Point out that although Josiah's repentance was emotional, it wasn't *only* emotional. He immediately followed it up with actions that expressed his new convictions.

5. HOW CAN WE RESPOND WRONGLY TO GOD'S DISCIPLINE?

This page presents many opportunities for lively discussion. For example, ask your class to put themselves in God's place. Why would these negative responses be offensive to Him when His intentions in the disciplining process are loving and only for our best?

6. WHAT ARE THE POSITIVE WAYS WE SHOULD RESPOND TO GOD'S DISCIPLINE?

Talk Point. The moment we repent of our sin, God's discipline stops. But if we wrongly attribute the painful ongoing natural consequences of our sin to God, our love relationship with Him suffers. We feel unfairly "picked on," and we may be tempted to rebel and fall back into sin.

Key Point. At this juncture, if not sooner, students will likely raise an important question: _Is God's hand behind all the painful things that happen?_ The answer is no. We live in a fallen world. People hurt other people. And we're all affected by negative circumstances and destructive natural events. The overarching promise in the New Testament about trials is that, if we let Him, God will work through every circumstance to bless us (Romans 8:28). Every test, no matter how difficult, provides both an opportunity for us to respond more fully to His best for our life, and for others to see God's glory revealed in our actions (John 9:1–3).

7. WHAT CAN KEEP ME FROM RESPONDING POSITIVELY TO GOD'S DISCIPLINE?

Refer to week 1, section 7 for comments.

MY NEW START IN A LIFE OF REPENTANCE

Give your class several minutes to read the text and respond to the invitation. Turn the page for your closing prayer.

Week Three

PRUNING

HOW GOD MAKES ROOM FOR MORE OF THE BEST

Welcome. Report on the week: "How did our study about God's discipline affect your life during the last week?"

Getting Started. Read the introductory text aloud and review the week's objectives listed in the "This Week You'll Discover…" box. Then open with prayer. Ask God for new insights and fresh vision as you discover what it means to be pruned by God.

1. AM I A LEAF LOVER OR A FRUIT FANATIC?

Question 1. Because the word *priorities* is often an overused catch phrase in our culture, it's easy to miss its importance in our spiritual lives. The Bible never uses the word directly, but it addresses the subject of our priorities repeatedly. Ask your class to suggest words or phrases the Bible uses to talk about priorities—e.g., "seek first," "earnestly desire," "above all," "in everything you do," "where your treasure is," "this one thing," "lose your life," and "forsaking all else."

Inventory. Invite your group to share results. Acknowledge that the first four of the statements on the inventory paint a picture of a very devoted Christian indeed. Did anyone feel confident enough to mark all four with "Strongly agree"?

Talk Point. Ask the class if this inventory paints a picture of the kind of Christian they sincerely want to become. If so, they're going to love this week's study!

2. WHAT IS PRUNING, AND WHY DO I NEED IT?

Question 2. The key word in this question is *productive:* "*Every* branch that *bears fruit*…" That means 100 percent will be pruned.

Question 3. How does pruning help us to reorder our priorities? You might spend a few minutes talking about this in practical terms. For example, let's say that God is pruning you in the area of how you spend your free time. He might ask you to give up an hour of television so that you could commit to phone your unsaved and lonely grandmother every week during this time. You have just reprioritized and directed your resources toward bearing fruit, rather than leaves.

Question 4. The word *pruning,* used as a spiritual principle of how God changes us, occurs only once in the New Testament. But your students should be able to make an immediate link between pruning and the more familiar Bible teachings on tests and trials. Tests and trials are often simply the "how" of God's pruning work.

Questions 5 and 6. Ask your class to notice that both James and Peter find a direct link between this kind of trial and joy (James 1:2; 1 Peter 1:6). Have your students ever been surprised by joy in the middle of a time of testing? What did they learn from that experience?

Talk Point. It's easy to look at someone who has godly priorities and forget that this doesn't happen automatically or without sacrifice.

3. WHAT WILL PRUNING LOOK LIKE IN MY LIFE?

Question 1. [a.] Paul's trials resulted in advancing the gospel.

Question 2. *[a.]* Through pruning, Paul was able to say, "When I am weak, then I am strong" (v. 10). Pruning leads to a yielding of our whole selves, including our weaknesses and self-reliance, which makes more room for God and His strength to be at work in us.

Question 3. If time permits, ask the class, "If pruning is only as effective as we permit, how do you suppose we might oppose God's efforts?" (Later, we'll talk more about our response to God's pruning.)

Question 4. Speculate with the class about why God allows trials to last beyond what we think we can endure. One answer is that in a test of your faith, your ability to trust God doesn't grow until you've been pushed beyond your present comfort zone.

WHAT OTHER BIBLE PEOPLE SHOW HOW GOD PRUNES US?

ABRAHAM

Question 3. God doesn't want us to surrender our loved ones to Him so He can hurt them; rather, it is so we aren't hindered in any way from serving Him. What other benefits do we experience when we surrender our loved ones to God's keeping? Invite any who are willing to share personal experiences.

Question 4. Encourage the class to ask themselves what practical things they might do or say to God in order to lay their "Isaac" on His altar.

JOSEPH

Question 1. God wants us to surrender even our dreams to Him. He asks us to trust in His timing and His plan, rather than try to make things happen in the way and time frame we deem best.

Question 2. *[a.]* God was with him. *[b.]* God showed him kindness. *[c.]* God granted him favor with the prison warden.

Question 3. What others intend for evil, God intends for good to accomplish His purposes. Ask the class to consider how knowing this truth might help in times of pruning.

Talk Point. Assure the class that when someone has been unjust or hurtful in the past, it wasn't necessarily God's will. However, God ultimately can use even sins committed against us for our good, if we're willing (Romans 8:28).

HOW CAN I GET THE MOST OUT OF PRUNING?

Give your class several minutes to study this chart.

Key Point. As your students process the information in the comparison chart, they may still be uncertain about what season they're in. If so, tell them to follow four steps that I have found useful with audiences around the world:

[1.] Acknowledge that God is trying to get your attention on an important issue.

[2.] Believe that, like a good parent, your loving Father would want you to know why He is intervening in your life.

[3.] Pray out loud: *Lord, do I have a major sin that's causing You to discipline me?* Ask Him to show you within a week if it is discipline; otherwise, you will take it by faith that you are in pruning. Tell Him that you are precommitting to obey His leading.

[4.] Relax in the knowledge that God *will* show you the truth.

Question 1. Some students may feel uncomfortable speculating. Assure them that this question isn't intended to encourage them to go around diagnosing others. It is intended to help them consider the general spiritual state of their faith community and what pruning or chastening might look like from an onlooker's perspective. God doesn't chasten and prune only individuals. We know from Scripture that God also chastens and prunes churches, ministries, cities, and even nations.

Talk Point. Some examples: "This means you're doing something right," "Someday, all this discomfort is going to really pay off," "I can see that God is shaping you into the person you really want to be," and "Pruning now means you have an awesome harvest for God in your future."

6. RESPONDING FOR RESULTS

Question 1. Rest.

Question 2. Rejoice. *[a.]* When we choose to rejoice, we are telling God and others that we believe in God's spiritual work in us and that we see a bigger picture than the one that's visible right now. Our joy in trials is evidence of our hope in God and a witness to unbelievers. Peter wrote, "Always be ready to give a defense to everyone who asks you a reason for the hope that is in you" (1 Peter 3:15).

Ask the class to consider: Does *not* taking joy in trials help or hurt your ability to bear them?

Question 3. Relinquish. *[a.]* Some possible reasons: We don't trust God; we mistakenly believe that the pleasure we derive from that to which we cling is greater than the pleasure of yielding to God; we misunderstand God's ways or suspect His motives; we think He'll give up and go away if we resist long enough.

DO I NEED TO APOLOGIZE TO GOD?

Be sure to direct your class's attention to this very important message.

7. WHAT IS KEEPING ME FROM SURRENDERING TO GOD'S PRUNING?

Refer to week 1, section 7 for comments.

MY NEW START IN SURRENDERING TO GOD

Give your class several minutes to read the text and respond to the invitation. Turn the page for your closing prayer.

Week Four

ABIDING

HOW GOD INVITES YOU
TO FLOURISH IN HIS PRESENCE

Welcome. Report on the week: "Did you find yourself thinking differently about your priorities? Did anyone make changes in this area that they'd like to share?"

Getting Started. Read the introductory text aloud and review the week's objectives listed in the "This Week You'll Discover…" box. Then open with prayer. Ask God to show your class how to break through to a significantly deeper relationship with Him.

1. WHAT DO I BELIEVE ABOUT GETTING CLOSE TO GOD?

Question 1. Follow up on students' answers to help them discover whether these experiences resulted—at least in part—from something *they* did to move closer to God. *Inventory.* All but fairly new Christians will probably find it pretty easy to answer "Strongly disagree" to these beliefs. But what we know in our heads often doesn't translate to the deep level of belief that dictates our actions. Invite the class to reexamine the inventory in terms of how they actually *operate* on a day-to-day basis. Do their results change?

2. WHAT DOES IT MEAN TO ABIDE?

Question 3. When we're not in close fellowship with God, it is never because God has moved, but because we have. We fail to "remain" when we neglect our relationship with Him or when we live in ongoing sin. Point out to the class the tenderness and urgency of Jesus' request that we "stay." Ask if they have ever begged someone not to leave them. What did that feel like?

If time permits, discuss how students respond to the different words that describe our personal connection with God: *friendship, intimacy, fellowship, communion,* and *abiding.* What connotations do these words carry? Which seem most doable?

Talk Point. The purpose of this talk point is to help students realize that yes, it is very possible to be "in Christ" but not to abide with Him on a relational level. This could be compared to how it's possible for a child to be estranged from a parent and not on speaking terms but still remain the parent's son or daughter, perhaps even living in the same house.

WELCOME TO THE PLACE OF ABIDING

Question 1. Jesus described a deep level of intimacy that supersedes what is possible in the physical realm. How does this amazing invitation make your class feel? How convinced are they that what Jesus describes is possible for ordinary Christians?

Question 2. [b.] Ask your class to notice how often Jesus refers to loving one another in John 15. To abide in God's love, we must obey His commands. The command He emphasizes here is to love one another. Loving one another, then, is one key to abiding. It also follows that when we abide in God's love, we will be much more capable of and inclined toward loving others.

Question 3. Some examples: reading His Word regularly; meditating on His Word; memorizing His Word; praying with words from the Bible.

3. WHY IS ABIDING SO IMPORTANT?

Question 1. [a.] and [b.] This passage is often used as an invitation to salvation. But in Revelation 3:20, Jesus was speaking to Christians. His invitation to "dine with him, and he with Me" would have resonated with His disciples, who treated mealtimes as important occasions for conversation. The fact that Jesus pictures Himself knocking, waiting to enjoy a shared meal, is a tender reminder that He hungers for intimate fellowship with us—and it's our move.

Question 2. [b.] Some examples: busyness with church activities; career success; having control and power; drugs, alcohol, or other addictions; sex; raising great kids; acquiring money. *[c.]* Encourage the class to discuss possible reasons we might lack the desire for intimacy with God. Some possibilities might include: We haven't ever tasted what's possible; we are too busy trying to get fulfilled in other ways; we are afraid to come face-to-face with Him; we don't recognize our spiritual hunger for what it is. Ask the class if they have ever considered *praying* that God would give them a great hunger for intimacy with Him; then challenge them to do so.

Question 3. Another way to phrase this question might be: Why might the youth pastor who is prepared and abides for an hour with God before meetings be more effective than one who comes prepared but doesn't abide at all?

4. HOW DOES ABIDING LEAD TO "MUCH" FRUIT?

Question 1. [b.] No matter what season we're in, the source of our fruitfulness is our connection to God. If a branch is separated from the vine and lying on the ground, how much fruit will it produce? Not one grape! This is a reminder that all our good works come from His power at work in us as we cooperate *with* Him, not from striving in our own strength apart from Him.

Question 2. First, read the "Miracle of More for Less" box aloud. Then challenge your class to take time and really process the question posed here. Ask for volunteers who are willing to share their answers.

WHO ELSE IN THE BIBLE
CHOSE TO ABIDE?

MARY

Question 2. It's easy to approach our time with God as a task to do, rather than an opportunity to meet with a Person. Speculate with your class about how it would change their quiet times with God if He were actually sitting in the room with them. *Question 3.* Ask the class if they really believe every Christian is not only called to abide, but equally *able* to do so. Suggest to the class that even though we may face unique obstacles (circumstances, abilities, or personality traits), we can all look for creative personal ways to learn to abide.

HOW DO I
GROW IN ABIDING?

Question 3. *[a.] through [e.]* Give the class time to quietly work through this list in groups of two or three. Afterward, point out that it is possible to do every one of these disciplines without abiding—but it's not possible to abide for long without them. Discuss the difference between going through the motions of the disciplines as a program and actually using them as tools to encounter a Person.

Assure students that the inventory part of the page was not intended to be guilt-inducing but eye-opening. Ask volunteers to share results or reactions. Ask the group if they believe it is possible to be very intimate with Jesus without practicing these disciplines. Why or why not?

WHAT CAN KEEP ME
FROM ABIDING?

Refer to week 1, section 7 for comments.

MY NEW START IN ABIDING

Give your class several minutes to read the text and respond to the invitation. Turn the page for your closing prayer. Thank your class for the time and effort they've invested in this important study. You may want to suggest several follow-up plans for individuals or groups:

[1.] Find an accountability partner who will help you process a discipline or pruning or abiding issue you're dealing with.

[2.] Form a support group of class members who want to grow in their spiritual discipline in the months ahead.

[3.] Gather as a group to view the *Secrets of the Vine Video Series,* available from Walk Thru the Bible Ministries and Multnomah Publishers.

Have various members share with the class what God has done in their lives through studying *Secrets of the Vine.* Share your testimony at blessings@prayerofjabez.com.

Introduction

THE PICTURE OF TRUE ABUNDANCE

I f you were to choose one picture to show what God wants from your life, what would it be? A truckload of success? A houseful of happiness? A mountain of hard work for Him?

If you've read *Secrets of the Vine,* you know that on the night before He died, Jesus gave His disciples a remarkable word picture. He wanted to show them what they had been chosen to accomplish. And even more, He wanted them to see and remember what their actively and intimately involved God would do to help bring it into being.

Jesus chose a dramatic moment—the night before His crucifixion. After their last meal together, Jesus led His friends through Jerusalem's darkened streets, outside the city walls, toward Gethsemane, where betrayal and arrest awaited Him. On the way, they walked through an ancient vineyard. Here, I believe, Jesus paused.

LEANING CLOSE TO LISTEN

His disciples gathered expectantly in the circle of torchlight. What would their Lord tell them now, on the night before His death? They leaned forward to hear. Then Jesus began a most surprising conversation.

> "I AM THE TRUE VINE, AND MY FATHER IS THE VINEDRESSER. EVERY
> BRANCH IN ME THAT DOES NOT BEAR FRUIT HE TAKES AWAY; AND
> EVERY BRANCH THAT BEARS FRUIT HE PRUNES, THAT IT MAY BEAR
> MORE FRUIT. I AM THE VINE, YOU ARE THE BRANCHES. HE WHO ABIDES
> IN ME, AND I IN HIM, BEARS MUCH FRUIT.... BY THIS MY FATHER IS
> GLORIFIED, THAT YOU BEAR MUCH FRUIT." (JOHN 15:1–2, 5, 8)

Imagine with me how these words must have sounded to Jesus' friends. Instead of talking about how they could defeat the Romans, Jesus talked to them about a grapevine and its branches. Instead of unveiling an escape plan, Jesus spoke resolutely about bearing fruit—a lot of it. Instead of saying good-bye, Jesus made it clear that an ongoing, vital relationship with Him would not only be possible, but would also be the key to breaking through to the highest yield possible.

His thoughts were on fruit, more fruit…*much* fruit. My friend, that's what this Bible study is about, too—and that is the picture God sees for your life!

A DIFFERENT KIND OF BIBLE STUDY

The four-week Bible study you're holding invites you to go deeply into God's Word to see how Jesus' teaching on fruitfulness, found in John 15, is supported and explained by the whole of Scripture. Besides being biblically based and felt-needs oriented, the study has several key distinctives:

It's topical. We focus on the biblical ways to seek and experience greater spiritual fruitfulness so that we can do God's work in the world. You won't find, for example, a book study or an in-depth approach to theology or doctrine.

It's conversation friendly. Some questions are information based. Some are intended simply to provoke a helpful discussion.

It's designed for individual or group use.

It's question driven. Sometimes called the Socratic method, this teaching method pulls you from topic to topic through a sequence of key questions.

It incorporates several learning approaches. You'll find inductive studies, fill-in-the-blanks, personal inventories, character profiles, Bible exposition, activity-based assignments, and inspiring quotes.

It offers optional study plans. The study presents more learning opportunities than a class can complete in an hour. Select the material that will work best for you. Some groups will want to extend this four-part study to an eight- or twelve-week course.

It's all about life change. The whole purpose of studying God's Word is to be changed in our character and our behavior so that we please God more, become more like Christ, and serve Him more every day.

BIBLE VERSION

The study, as well as the book it is based on, has been prepared using the New King James Version of the Bible. Using that version privately or in class will ensure convenience and clarity, but it is not required.

BREAK THROUGH TO THE FRUITFUL LIFE

If you're like most Christians, you may be shocked to learn how actively God pursues fruitfulness in your life. In fact, most Christians are unaware of what God is up to in their lives and therefore remain in the dark about how they can cooperate with Him for results.

But I promise you that by the time you complete the *Secrets of the Vine Bible Study,* you'll know exactly where you are in your spiritual life and what you can do today to break through to the next level of fruitfulness for God.

HELPING YOU GET AROUND

You'll see three icons used throughout the study to help you use the material more quickly.

 indicates a key verse, definition, or explanation that you won't want to miss.

 indicates optional material for further study. Use this icon to help you decide what materials you can leave for later.

 *indicates a group process question that focuses on life experience.*

RECOMMENDED RESOURCES

♦ *Secrets of the Vine Audio,* read by the author, can provide busy people with an easy way to learn and review the message of the book.

♦ *Secrets of the Vine Devotional* (and accompanying *Journal*) by Bruce Wilkinson. This thirty-one-day devotional follows the same four-week structure as the Bible study.

♦ If you are a teenager (or have one in your home), I recommend *Secrets of the Vine for Teens.*

♦ For children, see the Tommy Nelson products featured in the back of this book.

♦ Visit www.secretsofthevine.com for recent updates from author and publisher, new product updates, inspiring stories from readers, and other information.

♦ Also watch for the *Secrets of the Vine Video Series,* available soon from Walk Thru the Bible Ministries and Multnomah Publishers.

If you haven't read *Secrets of the Vine* yet, I highly recommend that you do so right away. You'll benefit even more from your Bible discoveries if you've personally encountered the life-changing truths of the book this study is based on. I also encourage you to enhance your learning experience each day for the next month by following along in the *Secrets of the Vine Devotional* and *Secrets of the Vine Journal.*

As you move from page to page in the days ahead, remember that God didn't just save you from death; He saved you for a specific and important life. And as you listen closely to Jesus' words, you'll discover exactly what that is. May God bless you *abundantly!*

—*Bruce Wilkinson*

FRUITFULNESS

WHAT GOD WANTS FROM THE BRANCH OF YOUR LIFE

> "You did not choose Me,
> but I chose you and appointed
> you that you should go
> and bear fruit, and that your
> fruit should remain."
>
> JOHN 15:16

RECOMMENDED READING

Secrets of the Vine, Chapters 1–2
Secrets of the Vine Devotional, Week 1

GETTING STARTED

What if God chose you for a specific and important mission, but you didn't know what it was?

What if God was at work in your life to help you succeed in your mission, but because you didn't understand His ways, you spent a lot of time and energy sabotaging your own future?

Talk about wasted potential! Unfortunately, too many Christians find themselves in just such a predicament. But there's good news. Jesus gave us a memorable picture of exactly what God expects from our lives, how He is at work *right now* to make it happen, and how we can cooperate to see extraordinary results.

In this Bible study, we're going to explore what Jesus told His best friends in a vineyard the night He was betrayed. His topic was fruitfulness. That may not be a word you've used before to describe your life, but it's a subject that was foremost in Jesus' mind that night.

You see, God didn't just save you *from* judgment and death. He saved you *to* a wonderful and important life. He wants your life to produce a life-harvest for Him today. It's a mission that will make a difference for eternity. And, as you'll discover, your greatest personal fulfillment will come when you reach for it with all your heart.

THIS WEEK YOU'LL DISCOVER...

- ◆ what God wants you to produce with your life.
- ◆ what the Bible means by "fruitfulness."
- ◆ how important your fruitfulness is to God.
- ◆ how proactive God is in your life today to help you succeed at your mission of fruitfulness.
- ◆ the four different levels of fruitfulness for believers.
- ◆ what you can do to cooperate with God's amazing plan.

1. WHAT DO I BELIEVE ABOUT WHAT MY LIFE SHOULD "PRODUCE" FOR GOD?

1. *What have you accomplished in your life so far that might be eternally important from God's point of view? Why did you pick what you did?*

MY LIFE HARVEST INVENTORY

2. *The following Life Harvest Inventory will reveal what you believe to be true about what you're supposed to produce for God. Score yourself using this standard:*
    ❶ Strongly disagree. ❷ Slightly disagree. ❸ Unsure. ❹ Agree. ❺ Strongly agree.

____ Accepting Christ is just the beginning of God's plans for my life.

____ God wants my life to add up to a *significant* harvest for His kingdom.

____ God wants me to know what He expects from my life and to understand how to cooperate with Him every day.

____ Trying hard to stay busy and productive doesn't guarantee that I'm pleasing God or that I'm doing what really counts for eternity.

____ God wants me to live up to my potential life harvest so much that He will intervene in my life to help me produce a big crop.

____ YOUR SCORE: Total the values assigned to the five statements. If you scored...

21–25 PRIZEWINNING HARVEST.
    You can expect a bumper crop.

16–20 PROMISING CROP.
    You're headed for a good showing.

11–15 POOR PICKINGS.
    You're a little confused about how to get results

5–10 PLUM EMPTY.
    You need to make a change, and soon!

"**" TALK POINT "**"

Who do you know that is making a significant difference for God?

What is it about this person's life that seems so important?

What are some of the traits that you would like to have said about you?

2. WHAT IS GOD'S VINEYARD AND WHAT DOES IT MEAN FOR ME?

KEY 🔑 Read John 15:1–8. In His vineyard teaching, Jesus described a powerful word picture to show how God works to produce abundance in our lives. The image Jesus chose was that of a grape plant. He said:

"I am the vine,

　　you are the branches.

He who abides in Me,

　　and I in him,

　　bears much fruit;

for without Me

　　you can do nothing."

— JOHN 15:5

Jesus identified each element found in the vineyard:

1. THE VINE is _____ *(v. 1). In the vineyard, the vine is the main stem or trunk that grows up out of the ground.*

2. THE VINEDRESSER is God the _____ *(v. 1). A vinedresser cares for each branch in such a way that it produces the most grapes possible.*

3. THE BRANCH is a _____ *(v. 5). The branch grows out from the vine and produces leaves, shoots, and fruit.*

4. THE FRUIT doesn't grow on the vine, but on the _____ *(vv. 2, 5). A large harvest of fruit is the desired result from a well-tended vineyard.*

WHO'S IN THIS PICTURE?

Before we go further, let's look at what the Bible says about the three persons present in Jesus' portrait of the vineyard:

1. JESUS, THE VINE. Jesus was born to human parents but He—along with the Father and Holy Spirit—is God. He is God the Son.

    a. Jesus is the _____, the _____ of God (John 20:30–31).

    b. Jesus died for our _____, and after three days He _____ from the dead (1 Corinthians 15:3–4).

    c. Whoever _____ in Jesus Christ receives the forgiveness of sins and the gift of eternal life (John 3:16; 20:31).

2. THE FATHER, THE VINEDRESSER. God the Father is the unseen King of heaven. Along with the Son and the Holy Spirit, He is God.

    a. God the Father is the source of _____ (John 5:21).

    b. God is the _____ of our Lord Jesus Christ (1 Peter 1:3).

    c. The Father is called the God of all _____ (2 Corinthians 1:3–4) and the source of every _____ and _____ gift (James 1:17).

3. THE CHRISTIAN, THE "BRANCH IN ME." A branch in Christ is a person who has received the gift of salvation through faith in Jesus Christ (John 15:2, 5).

    a. Early Christians identified one another as those who were _____ Christ Jesus (1 Peter 5:14).

    b. There is no condemnation to those who are _____ Christ Jesus. (Romans 8:1).

    c. A person "in Christ" is a _____ creation (2 Corinthians 5:17).

3. WHAT QUALIFIES AS FRUIT?

KEY Fruit is not something you produce to earn salvation, which is a gift you receive through faith in Jesus Christ (Ephesians 2:8–10). Rather, fruit is something that you do as a Christian to meet a need and bring glory to God.

1. *Throughout the New Testament, the word* fruit *is used interchangeably with the words* good works. *For example, in Titus 3:*

    a. *Verses 7–8: As an heir of God, you should be _____ to maintain good works. These are things that _____others.*

    b. *Verse 14: Fruitfulness means that you are doing _____ and meeting urgent _____.*

2. *Can you imagine a more urgent need than spreading the Good News of Jesus Christ? Identify the two active components of the Great Commission in Mark 16:15:* "_____into all the world and _____the gospel to every creature."

3. *What good works that meet urgent needs do you find in the following passages?*

    ACTS 16:14–15

    2 CORINTHIANS 9:7–8

    2 TIMOTHY 4:5

    JAMES 1:27

    JAMES 5:14–15

4. *Write down an urgent need of someone you know. What can you do this week to make a difference for that person?*

> *Joy comes from seeing the complete fulfillment*
> *of the specific purpose for which I was created and born again,*
> *not from successfully doing something of my own choosing.*
>
> OSWALD CHAMBERS

5. Jesus affirms three very important fruits or good works that we do privately in our
    Christian lives. Find them in Matthew 6:1–4, 5–13, and 16–18:

    _____   _____   _____

6. In addition to meeting the needs of others, fruit can be an outward expression of the
    inner work of God in your character.

    a. Read Galatians 5:22–23, and list the nine fruits of the Spirit:

    _____ _____ _____ _____ _____

    _____ _____ _____ _____

    b. In this context, fruit is used to describe the Holy Spirit's work in us as we
       abide in Christ. How might expressing these qualities help us to bear fruit
       for God?

" " TALK POINT " "

The words *fruit that
remains* (John 15:16)
show that God
wants our yield to
have eternal value.
Can you think
of a few worthy
pursuits that may
not qualify as "fruit
that remains"? Why
did you choose
those examples?

7. Christians are also urged to work hard to develop
    godly character qualities. Read 2 Peter 1:5–8. Peter
    tells us to give "all diligence" to adding important
    personal traits to our faith. What is the purpose of
    this? See verse 8:

    a. For if these things are yours and abound, you
       will be neither _____
       nor _____ in
       the knowledge of our Lord Jesus Christ.

    b. What character quality do you need to give
       more diligence to in this season of your life?

If you decided to
focus on producing
fruit tomorrow,
in what area of
your life would you
start first?

4. HOW IMPORTANT IS IT FOR ME TO BEAR FRUIT?

Many Christians overemphasize *faith* in Christ and underemphasize *fruit* for Christ. The truth is that once we become followers of Christ, God commands us to bear fruit. As you'll see below, a life filled with lasting results is exactly what He created us to enjoy.

THE "GRAPE COMMISSION"

1. *Look again at this week's theme verse:*

   "YOU DID NOT CHOOSE ME, BUT I CHOSE YOU AND APPOINTED YOU THAT YOU SHOULD GO AND BEAR FRUIT, AND THAT YOUR FRUIT SHOULD REMAIN." (JOHN 15:16)

   Did you notice how Jesus describes His followers? Take the key actions words and personalize them:

   a. I am _____ and I am _____.

   b. God wants me to _____ and _____.

> **" » TALK POINT " »**
>
> Since God has planned ahead for us to carry out specific good works, what do you suppose are the consequences when we choose not to carry them out?
>
> What good works do you feel uniquely positioned and gifted to accomplish?

2. *Ephesians 2:10 reveals two more surprising facts:*

   FOR WE ARE HIS WORKMANSHIP, CREATED IN CHRIST JESUS FOR GOOD WORKS, WHICH GOD PREPARED BEFOREHAND THAT WE SHOULD WALK IN THEM. (EPHESIANS 2:10)

   a. I am God's _____, _____ in Christ Jesus for good works.

   b. God has prepared these works _____ so I can accomplish them.

3. *Since God has chosen and appointed you to bear fruit, fruit that no one else can produce exactly like you can, what degree of importance do you think you should place on fulfilling this commission in your lifetime?*

5. HOW MUCH FRUIT DOES GOD WANT OR EXPECT?

RESULTS MATTER!

KEY By now you understand that one of the reasons God created you is to bear fruit for His glory. But here is more news: God doesn't just want some fruit, He wants—and expects—a lot of it. Not just quality but quantity matters to God.

Does that surprise you? Some Christians think that as long as they're saved, God will be satisfied. But as we saw in Ephesians 2:10, we have been saved for an exciting purpose.

In John 15, Jesus reveals four levels of fruit bearing:

LEVEL 1. <u>NO FRUIT</u> (*"every branch in Me that does not bear fruit," v. 2*).
LEVEL 2. <u>FRUIT</u> (*"every branch that bears fruit," v. 2*).
LEVEL 3. <u>MORE FRUIT</u> (*"that it may bear more fruit," v. 2*).
LEVEL 4. <u>MUCH FRUIT</u> (*"bears much fruit," vv. 5, 8*).

1. *Clearly, God wants more fruit, not less, from us. Look at verse 8 again—"By this My Father is glorified, that you bear _____ _____." In fact, only for the category "much fruit" does Jesus emphasize that God receives glory.*

2. *Based on your observations, how would you rate the quantity of fruit in the life of the average Christian?*

NO FRUIT	FRUIT	MORE FRUIT	MUCH FRUIT
0 – 10 – 20 – 30 – 40 – 50 – 60 – 70 – 80 – 90 – 100			

3. *Based on your observations, how would you rate your own quantity of fruit?*

NO FRUIT	FRUIT	MORE FRUIT	MUCH FRUIT
0 – 10 – 20 – 30 – 40 – 50 – 60 – 70 – 80 – 90 – 100			

4. *How comfortable are you with placing a lot of emphasis on what you do or don't accomplish for God? If Jesus sat down today to talk with you about the quantity of fruit in your life, what do you think He would say?*

6. WHAT CAN I LEARN FROM A BIBLE CHARACTER ABOUT FRUITFULNESS?

PETER

Fishing for the Catch of a Lifetime

eXTRA The New Testament record of Peter's life gives us enough biographical information that we can see his progress from ordinary fisherman to extraordinary servant of God.

1. Peter was a fisherman from the lakeside town of Bethsaida. One day Jesus showed God's power to Peter and his fishing partners. After He told the men where to fish, they caught such a _____ of fish that their _____ began to break (Luke 5:6).

2. Then Jesus invited the men to do more than just make a living: "Follow Me, and I will make you _____ of _____" (Matthew 4:19).

3. Even though Peter had been personally taught and discipled by Jesus (Matthew 10:1), he sinned under pressure. Read Luke 22:56–62. What did he do?

4. After the Resurrection, Peter left God's calling and went back to fishing. Sin had stopped his fruitfulness. But Jesus came looking for him. Again, He miraculously provided an enormous catch of fish (John 21:1–6). What does this say to you about how earnestly God pursues us when we are in sin to bring us back to fruitfulness?

" " TALK POINT " "

Jesus didn't want Peter's failure to permanently disqualify him as a "fisher of men." What are three serious sins that you've seen keep people from living a productive life for God?

5. Later, Jesus asked Peter, "Do you love Me?" (see John 21:15–17). Each time Peter said yes, Jesus told him to care for His sheep. Jesus wanted Peter to realize that if he truly loved Him, Peter would do what Jesus had appointed him to do. Have you ever consciously measured your love for God by what you are willing to do for Him? Does this correlation make you uncomfortable? If so, why?

6. In Acts, Peter became the first leader of the church. God worked through him to bring an abundant harvest for eternity. List some fruits you can find in his ministry:

ACTS 2:38–41 _____ ACTS 3:1–8 _____ ACTS 4:8–13 _____

ACTS 5:14–16 _____ ACTS 10:34–48 _____

7. Years later, Peter urged believers to live in such a way that nonbelievers might "by your good _____ which they observe, _____ God" (1 Peter 2:11–12).

8. Read Matthew 5:16 (see box below). What are some good works that, when seen by others who do not know Christ, would make them thank God for His work in you?

SHINE OUT!

"Let your light so shine before men, that they may see your good works and glorify your Father in heaven."

—JESUS CHRIST, MATTHEW 5:16

7. WHAT CAN KEEP ME FROM A FRUITFUL LIFE?

KEY John 15 is full of surprises for many Christians and calls for significant changes in how a person goes about living his life. But change is hard, especially when we let ourselves stay trapped in wrong thinking. The following are misconceptions about the fruitful life; choose the responses that most seem to be hindering you from making a change today. Let the Bible help you discover a new breakthrough truth, and write it down (in your own words) in the space provided.

EXCHANGING BARREN FOR BOUNTIFUL

☐ TOO ORDINARY. *I'm not especially gifted, so how can God expect my life to produce eternal results?* I Corinthians 12:7, 11; Ephesians 2:10; I Peter 4:10–11.

☐ TOO BUSY. *I'm already overwhelmed just making ends meet and doing what has to be done. I don't have time to bear fruit for God.* Luke 12:22–31; I Timothy 4:8.

☐ TOO DISCOURAGED. *Every time I try to do more for God, I fall on my face. I don't want to try again.* Romans 15:13; 2 Corinthians 12:9–10; Galatians 6:7–10; James 5:7.

☐ TOO INDIFFERENT. *Seems like fruitfulness matters just for religious professionals like pastors and missionaries—and that's not me.* Ephesians 4:11–16; I Timothy 6:18–19; Hebrews 10:23–25; I Peter 2:9.

☐ TOO INEXPERIENCED. *I want to do great things for God but I don't have the right background or training.* Zechariah 4:6; I Corinthians 1:20–31; I Timothy 4:12–16.

My New Breakthrough Belief:

_____

_____

_____

_____

_____

My New Start in a Fruitful Life

The decision to make your life all about bearing fruit for God is a momentous one. If you take that step, your life will never be the same. The way you shape your priorities—even the way you pursue God—will change dramatically. But as producing results for God becomes a great passion in life, you'll overflow with the joy that comes from doing exactly what you were created to do.

And here's the best news. God doesn't send you out to do good works for His glory in your own strength. He makes His power available to you. As you abide in Jesus the Vine, God will be at work to continually increase the flow of His love and power through you, His branch, to the whole world. This is the great and amazing purpose for which He saved you. Will you say yes?

TAKE A MOMENT TO RECORD YOUR NEW INSIGHTS.

As you read this chapter, what was your heart telling you?

Have you found throughout your life that you could do more for God, and that you wanted to do more? Have you decided to focus your life on bearing more fruit? If so, why?

Write your commitment in the box below. Sign your statement. Then turn the page for a closing prayer of commitment.

My personal decision to bear fruit for God in my life:

Signature   Date

My Prayer for Fruitfulness

Dear Lord,
Thank You that You have created and commissioned me
to bear a tremendous yield of fruit for You in my lifetime.
What an amazing destiny! Father, I reach now
for this destiny with all my heart. I don't want to miss
a single opportunity to do the good works You have prepared
for me to do. Forgive me, Lord, for letting distractions
and deceptions pull me away from Your wonderful plan.
I invite You as the Vinedresser to shape the branch of my life
in whatever way You desire so that I will yield a greater
and greater harvest for Your glory. Grant me Your grace
and power to accomplish this. Teach me in the days ahead
how to cooperate with You, not fight against You.
And I will praise You, from whom all blessings flow.
Amen.

For we are His workmanship, created in Christ Jesus for good works,
which God prepared beforehand that we should walk in them.

EPHESIANS 2:10

Week Two

DISCIPLINE

HOW GOD MOVES YOU FROM
BARREN TO BOUNTIFUL

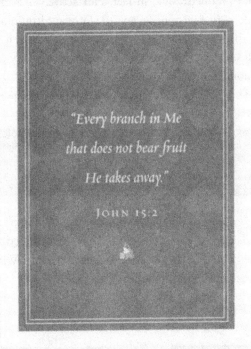

"*Every branch in Me
that does not bear fruit
He takes away.*"

JOHN 15:2

RECOMMENDED READING

Secrets of the Vine, Chapters 3–4
Secrets of the Vine Devotional, Week 2

GETTING STARTED

Now you know that you've been created and chosen for an incredibly fruitful life, a life that produces results that will count for eternity. And you've decided that's the life you deeply desire.

But what if there's no fruit in your life to speak of right now? What if you look back over the last weeks or even years of your life and still don't find much fruitfulness for God?

There's encouraging news for you! As you'll discover this week, Jesus cares so much about your fruitfulness that He will intervene to help you reach for a meaningful and productive life. In fact, He's actively at work behind the scenes of your life *right now* to bring you to abundant fruitfulness.

We'll learn this week how God intervenes in our lives if we choose to live in sin. We'll see, too, that He will increase the intensity of His actions if we fail to respond positively.

The Bible word for this restoration process—*discipline*—is the subject of the first secret of the vine.

> ### THE FIRST SECRET OF THE VINE
> *When we choose to waste our lives in sin, God intervenes through the process of discipline to convince us to stop sinning and begin bearing fruit again.*

The word *discipline* doesn't mean punishment. It doesn't refer to some kind of spiritual exercise program, either. Instead, it describes how God the Father lovingly intervenes when we stray into trouble. Why? So we can thrive like we were created to!

THIS WEEK YOU'LL DISCOVER...

+ what keeps your Christian life fruitless.
+ what negative consequences result from a fruitless life—and what you can do to make them stop.
+ how the Bible defines the word *discipline*.
+ what God's motives and methods are in discipline.
+ what level of discipline you might be in right now.
+ how to respond so God's discipline ends—and fruitfulness begins!

1. WHAT DO I BELIEVE ABOUT GOD'S INVOLVEMENT IN MY LIFE?

1. Can you describe a time when you weren't living the way God wanted you to but sensed that He was at work to motivate you to return to Him? Why did you come to this conclusion? What happened?

MY "BELIEFS ABOUT GOD'S INTERVENTION" INVENTORY

2. You may not know what you really believe about how involved God is in your life. Score your views using this standard: ❶ Strongly agree. ❷ Agree. ❸ Unsure. ❹ Slightly disagree. ❺ Strongly disagree.

____ I believe God doesn't intervene in the circumstances and events of my life.

____ I think God gives me freedom to obey Him or not. If I choose to go my own way, He respects my choice and stays out of the way.

____ I can't recall a time when I felt God directly respond when I sinned.

____ God is too kind and loving to bring corrective action when Christians get off track spiritually.

____ Some of my failings are just part of my personality. God knows I'm only human.

____ YOUR SCORE: Total the values above. If you scored…

21–25 CONVINCED. You know that God is actively involved in your life.

16–20 CONSCIOUS. You're pretty sure, most of the time, that God is actively involved in your life.

11–15 CONFUSED. You can't decide what you believe about God being actively involved in your life.

5–10 CLUELESS! You're in the dark about God's actions in your life.

3. If you were to discover that some of the distress in your life is a result of God's discipline because of your disobedience, would you be surprised? How would you respond? Does this feel promising or threatening to you?

2. HOW DOES GOD RESPOND WHEN MY LIFE IS UNPRODUCTIVE?

1. *John 15:2 gives us the answer. Write out the verse here:*

KEY A more precise translation of the Greek verb *airo*—here rendered "takes away"—would be "take up" or "lift up." Airo is the same word Jesus used when He told the lame man, "Take up your bed, and go to your house" (Matthew 9:6; see also Matthew 14:20; 16:24). In the vineyard, a grape branch does not bear fruit when it becomes diseased and barren and falls into the dirt. But the branch is too valuable to cut off. So a vinedresser "takes up" the branch, cleans it off, and refastens it to the trellis. Soon it's thriving again.

In the vineyard,
a grape branch does not
bear fruit when it becomes
diseased and barren
and falls into the dirt.

In a similar fashion, when a Christian becomes dirty and unproductive because of sin, God acts to lift him up and clean him off. The Bible calls this process discipline, which is described in the first secret of the vine: When we choose to waste our lives in sin, God intervenes through the process of discipline to convince us to stop sinning and begin bearing fruit again.

2. *How closely does the tender image of God cleansing you from sin and "lifting you up" correspond with your own experience? How might it change the way you view God's discipline?*

3. *What would you say is the longest you've gone in your life without any spiritual results to show for it?*
   ❑ *A day* ❑ *A week* ❑ *A month* ❑ *A year* ❑ *More than a year*

UNDERSTANDING GOD'S MOTIVES IN DISCIPLINE

1. *The goal of God's discipline of the believer is always for a person's good. According to the Bible, a man who withholds discipline actually "hates his son" (Proverbs 13:24). Read Hebrews 12:5–11. What do we learn about God's methods and motives in the disciplining process?*

    a. He disciplines us because He_____us (v. 6).

    b. He disciplines us as our Father because we are His _____ (v. 7).

    c. He doesn't discipline just some sons but _____ son (vv. 6–7).

    d. At the time, His discipline doesn't feel good; it feels _____ (v. 11).

    e. However, the purpose of His discipline is always for our _____ (v. 10).

    f. In fact, if we allow God to train us, the benefit is extraordinary: We become partakers of His _____ (v. 10) and receive the peaceable fruit of_____ (v. 11).

2. *According to verses 9–10, what are the differences between God's perfect discipline and imperfect human discipline? Why might those differences be very important to keep in mind?*

"" TALK POINT ""

How would you compare the parental discipline you received growing up to what you're learning about God's discipline? Do you think your past experiences in discipline influence your response to God today? If so, how?

PROOF OF THE VINEDRESSER'S DELIGHT

Whom the LORD loves He corrects,
just as a father the son in whom he delights.

PROVERBS 3:12

3. WHAT DOES GOD DO WHEN HE DISCIPLINES ME?

KEY As every parent understands, there's a big difference in how you discipline a child who doesn't make his bed and a child who repeatedly steals. Restorative discipline is always in proportion to the seriousness of the sin. Jesus taught the principle of escalating discipline in human relationships in Matthew 18:15–17. God disciplines us in the same way. In Hebrews 12, we find three levels of discipline.

THREE LEVELS OF GOD'S DISCIPLINE

LEVEL 1: REBUKE (v. 5). *A rebuke is a verbal warning. We receive God's rebukes:*
a. *Through our* _____ *(John 8:9).*
b. *By the truth of* _____ *(2 Timothy 3:16–17).*
c. *From a person who has spiritual authority in our lives—for example, a* _____ *, like Timonty (2 Timothy 2:24–26; 2 Timothy 4:2).*
d. *By the Holy* _____ *(John 16:7–8).*

LEVEL 2: CHASTEN (v. 6). *This word is used broadly in Scripture to describe the process of child-rearing, but it is often focused specifically on correction. In this text, since chasten is described as "painful" (v. 11), it indicates more intensive discipline than rebuke. Chastening results in anxiety, frustration, or distress. How would you describe chastening based on the use of the word in Psalm 118:18?*

LEVEL 3: SCOURGE (v. 6). *Scourging causes extreme physical pain. The same word is used to describe how soldiers whipped Jesus before His crucifixion (John 19:1). A New Testament example of scourging is found in 1 Corinthians 11:27–31. List the three serious negative consequences of God's discipline in verse 30.*

a. _____

b. _____

c. _____

" " TALK POINT " "

Have you understood before now that God will actually increase the intensity of His discipline if you don't respond? If a person really believed this, why would he persist in a serious sin?

COMPARING THE LEVELS OF DISCIPLINE

1. Do the following descriptions of how God disciplines us ring true for you? What additional details would you add from your own experience?

ISSUE	LEVEL 1. REBUKE	LEVEL 2. CHASTEN	LEVEL 3. SCOURGE
LEVEL OF INTENSITY	Light	Medium	Severe
HOW GOD GETS YOUR ATTENTION	Verbal	Emotional	Physical
WHAT YOU FEEL	Annoyance	Anguish	Agony
YOUR SPIRITUAL STATE	Under Conviction	In Conflict	In Crisis

2. Can you identify times in your life when you were in each of these three stages of discipline? What were the signs? How did you resolve the issues?

3. If you think you are in discipline now, which level seems to best describe your experience? Based on what you've learned, what can you expect to experience in your life if you continue in the direction you're going?

JUST SAY THE WORD...

Rebuke a wise man, and he will love you.
Give instruction to a wise man, and he will be still wiser.

PROVERBS 9:8–9

4. WHO ELSE IN THE BIBLE EXPERIENCED GOD'S DISCIPLINE?

Meet two promising leaders in the Bible. Both came to a personal "you-turn" as a result of God's discipline. One chose to charge ahead and suffered the painful consequences; the other repented and received the benefits of obedience.

CASE STUDY #1
Asa, the king who refused God's correction.

[Read 2 Chronicles 16:7–13]

Asa was a good king who initiated many reforms. In his later years, however, he began trusting in the power of his godless allies more than in God. When a prophet confronted him, King Asa refused to repent and angrily threw the prophet in prison. His life went downhill from there.

1. *Describe the escalating degrees of discipline you find in Asa's life in this passage:*
   a. *Rebuke (16:7–9):* _____ .
   b. *Chastening (16:10):* _____ .
   c. *Scourging (16:12):* _____ .

2. *Has God ever rebuked you through someone else's words? How did you respond?*

3. *How might Asa's life have turned out differently if he had responded to God's first degree of discipline?*

" " TALK POINT " "

Have you ever known someone who seemed to slide further and further away from God, even though he had many chances to turn things around?

What eventually happened to him?

TAKING IT TO EXTREMES

The Bible records other cases in which disobedience led God's people into disaster. Two examples: Saul, in 1 Samuel 13:1–14; and Ananias and Sapphira, in Acts 5:1–16.

CASE STUDY #2
Josiah, the king who responded to God's correction.

[Read 2 Kings 22:1–23:3]

e XTRA Like Asa, Josiah was a good king who initiated many reforms. During his reign, temple workers discovered a copy of the Book of the Law (a part of the first five books of the Bible). When a reading showed the king how far God's people had strayed, Josiah immediately repented.

1. *What tool did God use to reveal His impending severe discipline on the nation? (See 22:11, 19.)*

2. *Clearly, Josiah's personal repentance was deeply felt (22:18–19). Have you ever responded to God's discipline with a similar intensity of emotion? What did you learn from that turning point?*

3. *Josiah's repentance resulted in a historic spiritual turnaround for the nation (chapter 23). Have you discovered in your own life that when you genuinely repented of a sin, God gave you power to bear fruit right away? If so, what happened?*

" " TALK POINT " "

The intensity of Josiah's repentance is rarely seen in today's churches. Why do you think this is so?

What effect might this be having on the level of fruitfulness in our times?

*Harsh discipline is for him who forsakes the way,
and he who hates correction will die.*

PROVERBS 15:10

5. HOW CAN WE RESPOND WRONGLY TO GOD'S DISCIPLINE?

KEY You can probably recall a time in your own childhood when your response to parental discipline was anything but helpful. You sulked. You argued. You raged. The result? The good purpose of your parents' discipline in your life did not materialize.

Our key text of Hebrews 12:5–15 reveals both positive and negative responses to God's discipline.

<u>FIRST NEGATIVE RESPONSE</u>: *"Do not _____ the chastening of the LORD" (v. 5).*

> a. *When you despise how a person treats you, how do you tend to react?*

> b. *What could despising God's discipline look like in a person's actions, attitudes, or conversations?*

<u>SECOND NEGATIVE RESPONSE</u>: *"Nor be _____ when you are rebuked by Him" (v. 5).*

> a. *Why might a person feel discouraged when God's discipline occurs?*

> b. *What practical steps could you take to ward off discouragement when God is disciplining you?*

<u>THIRD NEGATIVE RESPONSE</u>: *"Looking carefully...lest any root of _____ springing up cause trouble" (v. 15).*

> a. *How have you witnessed a bitter response to God's discipline negatively affect yourself or others?*

> b. *What helpful things could you say to a person who is struggling with bitterness because of God's discipline?*

6. WHAT ARE THE POSITIVE WAYS WE SHOULD RESPOND TO GOD'S DISCIPLINE?

If you're in discipline, God wants it to stop even more than you do. But you are the one who decides when it ends. While the consequences may continue, God's discipline for a specific sin stops when you stop sinning. I hope you recognize the following positive responses to God's discipline in your own Christian experience.

FIRST POSITIVE RESPONSE: *"If you _____ chastening..." (v.7).*
God's chastening can last for a period of time. When a deeply-held value, habit, or character quality is the problem, change usually takes time. What convictions about God's character would help you endure painful circumstances for long periods of time?

SECOND POSITIVE RESPONSE: *"Be in _____to the Father" (v. 9).*
Submission is a deeper level of response. We learn to respect and be in subjection to our earthly fathers. How can the same attitude bring good results from God's discipline? Is there anything God is asking you to submit to Him at this time?

THIRD POSITIVE RESPONSE: *Chastening yields fruit "to those who have been _____ by it" (v. 11). The best result of discipline is lasting, positive change. Name a change in your character that came as a result of allowing God to train you through challenging circumstances.*

> **" " TALK POINT " "**
>
> God's discipline for specific sin ends as soon as we repent, but what kinds of painful consequences might continue?
>
> Why is it important for us to differentiate between the pain of God's intervention and the pain of a natural consequence?

7. WHAT CAN KEEP ME FROM RESPONDING POSITIVELY TO GOD'S DISCIPLINE?

KEY 🔑 We never have to be enslaved by sin, repeating the same destructive patterns (Romans 6:11–12). But at times, our human thinking can hold us hostage to lies. Choose the false beliefs that most seem to be keeping you from making a change today. Let the Bible help you discover a new breakthrough truth, and write it down (in your own words) in the space provided.

OLD OBSTACLES, NEW BREAKTHROUGH BELIEFS

❑ THE "I CAN OUTLAST GOD" STRATEGY. *You believe that God will eventually give up and leave you alone.* Psalm 139:7–12; Luke 15:1–7.

❑ THE "IF YOU CAN'T BEAT 'EM, JOIN 'EM" DEFENSE. *You believe that you can't give up your sin. You've tried many times; why try again?* Romans 6:14, 16, 18; 1 Corinthians 10:1–13; 2 Peter 2:9.

❑ THE "BIG, MEAN GOD" ASSUMPTION. *You believe that God is wrong to cause you pain no matter what you've done.* Job 5:17–18; Psalm 145:8–9; Ezekiel 33:11; Hebrews 12:5–17.

❑ THE "OSTRICH" MANEUVER. *You think that if you don't believe God will intervene, He probably won't.* Galatians 6:7–10; Philippians 2:12–13.

❑ THE "NO FIRE NOW MEANS NO FIRE LATER" GAMBLE. *You believe that if God doesn't discipline you immediately when you sin, He won't do anything later either.* Romans 2:4–11; 1 Corinthians 11:31–32; 2 Peter 3:1–9.

My New Breakthrough Belief:

_____

_____

_____

_____

_____

_____

_____

My New Start in a Life of Repentance

We've spent a week talking about serious matters. I understand if you arrive on this page feeling a little shaken. Perhaps you haven't been aware until now just how involved God is in the circumstances of your life, or that He would use discipline to convince you to let go of sin. But the very fact that you've had the courage to face these truths says that you want your life to count for eternity.

As we close this study, take a minute to record your reactions:

What has my emotional response been to learning that God actively disciplines me?

How has my thinking changed on this subject?

List some positive results you can expect to see as you commit to repenting quickly and completely when God disciplines you.

If you're ready, tell God in writing that you want to move forward into fruitfulness in your life. Tell Him the practical steps you'll take to respond to His will. Sign your statement. Then turn the page for a closing prayer of commitment.

My new commitment to responding to God's discipline:

Signature   *Date*

My Prayer to Respond to God's Discipline

Heavenly Father,
I understand now that sin has blighted my life
and kept me from producing fruit of lasting value for You.
I see that You have firmly and lovingly disciplined me to bring
me back to wholeness and abundance. Please forgive me
for my foolish rebellion. Now I wholeheartedly submit
to Your authority and will for me. I repent of my sin,
Lord, and I choose again to bear fruit for You.
From now on, I will endeavor to respond to
Your discipline quickly because I trust in Your goodness.
Teach me to obey, Lord! Fill my heart now
with great anticipation for the lasting harvest You will
accomplish in my life. Thank You!
Amen.

For the grace of God that brings salvation has appeared to all men, teaching us that,
denying ungodliness and worldly lusts, we should live soberly, righteously, and godly in
the present age, looking for the blessed hope and glorious appearing of our great God
and Savior Jesus Christ, who gave Himself for us, that He might redeem us from every
lawless deed and purify for Himself His own special people, zealous for good works.

TITUS 2:11–14

Week Three

PRUNING

HOW GOD MAKES ROOM
FOR MORE OF THE BEST

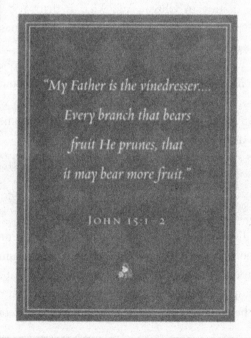

"My Father is the vinedresser....
Every branch that bears
fruit He prunes, that
it may bear more fruit."

JOHN 15:1–2

RECOMMENDED READING

Secrets of the Vine, Chapters 5–6
Secrets of the Vine Devotional, Week 3

GETTING STARTED

"Because the grape plant grows so vigorously, a lot of wood must be cut away each year. If you don't prune your plant, it will turn nearly all its energies to producing rampant growth rather than grapes...."

This advice from an old gardening manual introduces us to one of the most fascinating and powerful principles of fruit bearing: Greater fruitfulness never happens with unrestricted growth.

The process is called pruning. Jesus said, "Every branch that bears fruit He prunes, that it may bear more fruit" (John 15:2). Pruning means to thin, reduce, cut off. It's the way God shapes you and me so that we can fulfill our true destiny in Christ. And what is that? You and I are the Father's workmanship, created in Christ Jesus for fruitfulness, which God prepared for us in eternity past (Ephesians 2:10).

Last week we learned how God responds to the disobedient, barren branch so that it begins to bear fruit. The issue was sin, and the response God wanted from us was repentance. This week we look at what God does to move us from some or no fruit to the next level of fruitfulness: *more* fruit.

This leads us to the second secret of the vine.

> ## THE SECOND SECRET OF THE VINE
> *If your life bears some fruit, God will intervene from
> time to time to prune you so that you will bear more fruit.*

We'll also discover how to cooperate with God in this most promising season. For vigorous young branches, pruning can seem unnecessary and even counterproductive. But I've never met a mature Christian who didn't instinctively grasp the necessity and the amazing potential of pruning to help get us to the kind of life we want most but can't get to on our own.

THIS WEEK YOU'LL DISCOVER...

- ♦ what God does to the branch that bears fruit.
- ♦ the meaning of spiritual pruning.
- ♦ God's motives and methods in pruning.
- ♦ who else in the Bible experienced pruning.
- ♦ how to respond to God's pruning so that you can bear more fruit.

1. AM I A LEAF LOVER OR A FRUIT FANATIC?

1. *How successfully do you set priorities for your life from the perspective of what God wants? Do you see your priorities changing as you mature as a Christian?*

2. *Think of "leaves" as those things in your life, often even good things, that sap your energies, time, and talents but aren't ultimately important to God. Name a few.*

MY PRIORITIES INVENTORY

The following inventory will help you discover whether your current priorities are helping you to produce leaves or fruit for eternity. Score yourself using this standard: ❶ Strongly disagree. ❷ Slightly disagree. ❸ Unsure. ❹ Agree. ❺ Strongly agree.

____ I spend a lot of time and energy on activities that further God's kingdom.

____ I look for opportunities to use my gifts and talents in ways that will bring glory to God.

____ I am willing to undergo real change in order to shape my priorities to better match God's.

____ I can say with confidence that I put God before any person or possession.

____ I understand that busyness for God and acclaim from other believers aren't the same as spiritual productivity.

____ YOUR SCORE: Total the values above. If you scored...

21–25 PRIZEWINNING HARVEST. *Congratulations! Producing a huge harvest is of first importance for you.*

16–20 BUNCHES OF FRUIT. *Fruit matters to you, and you might be on the verge of a bumper crop.*

11–15 GRAPES HERE 'N' THERE. *Fruit is great when it happens, but life is busy!*

5–10 LEAF SALAD. *Unless things change, you're headed for the Leaf-Grower's Hall of Fame.*

" " **TALK POINT** " "

Which question on this inventory was the most difficult to answer, and why?

2. WHAT IS PRUNING, AND WHY DO I NEED IT?

To prune means to remove plant parts for a purpose. Gardeners prune to improve a plant's health or appearance, to increase the size of its blooms, or to produce more fruit. Pruning is always future oriented—the cutting now results in gains later.

Gardeners prune to improve

a plant's health or appearance,

to increase the size of its blooms,

or to produce more fruit.

1. Jesus said, "Every branch that bears fruit He prunes, that it may bear more fruit" (John 15:2). Based on this verse:
    a. Who does the pruning? _____
    b. What gets pruned? _____
    c. What is the goal of pruning? _____

2. This leads us to the second secret of the vineyard: If your life bears some fruit, God will intervene from time to time to prune you so that you will bear even more fruit. What percentage of productive Christians, therefore, should expect to be pruned?

3. Pruning helps us to reorder our priorities. What does Matthew 6:33 tell us was Christ's priority for His followers? Name three other priorities that often compete for the number one spot.

TALK POINT

Can you look back on a time when you felt compelled to change your priorities for the better? Did you recognize that it was God at work? Did it lead to more fruit?

THROW OFF EVERY WEIGHT

To love God is to throw off every spiritual weight
that will keep your soul from rising to Him.

AUGUSTINE OF HIPPO

4. When God prunes us it often takes place through tests and trials. The distress we experience helps us identify affections, activities, or attitudes that God is trying to prune. Have you ever experienced a trial that you later realized was directly related to your clinging to something that God was trying to prune away? Describe what happened.

5. Read James 1:2–5. What two benefits does James link to the testing of our faith?

    a. It produces _____ in the believer,

    b. which in turn promises to make us perfect and _____ .

6. Read 1 Peter 1:6–8. What key benefit ("more precious than gold") does Peter say results from testing?

    The _____ of

    your _____ .

7. How will knowing that God uses trials and tests to prune you and reshape your priorities change the way you respond to times of difficulty?

" " TALK POINT " "

Think of people whose priorities inspire you. What benefits do you see in their lives?

What challenging choices do you think their priorities require of them?

3. WHAT WILL PRUNING LOOK LIKE IN MY LIFE?

KEY 🔑 The apostle Paul allowed God to shape his life, and God used him to spread Christianity across the Roman world (Acts 9:15). From Paul's writings we can identify several important principles of pruning:

1. *The act of pruning is how God works in our lives when we're bearing fruit, and its goal is to bring us more fruit. Read Philippians 1:12–14.*
   a. *What kind of fruit came of Paul's trials?* _____.
   b. *Paul recognized the connection between his hardships and the fruit that resulted. Have you ever been able to make a similar correlation?*

2. *Pruning is always for our good and is custom-suited to our individual needs. Read 2 Corinthians 12:7–10.*
   a. *Paul allowed God to use his "thorn in the flesh" for greater ministry potential (v. 7). Looking back, do you see now how a personal limitation that you surrendered to God was used for greater fruitfulness? If so, what was it and what happened?*

   b. *How do you see God pruning you now in areas that correspond to how you feel personally called and gifted to serve Him?*

3. *Pruning is only as effective as we permit. Read Philippians 3:7–9.*
   a. *What is Paul's attitude toward losses he might endure in his quest to know Christ?* _____.
   b. *How would you compare Paul's attitude—his willingness to relinquish everything for Christ—with your own?*

WHERE GOD SHAPES US

Through pruning, God shapes our character and conduct. Here are some common focal points for His shears:

- ♦ Your commitment to God (Job 13:15).
- ♦ Your values (Matthew 6:19–21).
- ♦ Your money and possessions (Matthew 6:19–21, 24).
- ♦ Your gifts and talents (Matthew 25:14–30).
- ♦ Your relationships (Luke 14:26).
- ♦ Your sources of significance (2 Corinthians 4:7).
- ♦ Your time (Ephesians 5:15–16).

4. *Pruning can seem to go on longer than is fair or necessary. Read 2 Corinthians 1:8–11.*

  a. *What key response to extended trials does Paul reveal in verse 9?*

  _____.

  b. *Have you ever experienced a season of pruning so severe or prolonged that it forced you to rely completely on God? What happened?*

5. *Pruning is future-oriented—the loss happens now; the gain comes later. Look again at Galatians 6:9, which we studied in week 1.*

  a. *Paul encouraged the Galatians, who were facing many trials, not to grow weary in doing good works. But when does he say they—and we—shall reap the reward of our work?*

  b. *When you're being pruned, it's easy to get impatient for the harvest you know is coming. How confident are you that pruning will lead to abundance?*

" " TALK POINT " "

In pruning, God isn't taking away from us; He is shaping us into who He created us to be. Discuss the kind of person God longs for you to become. How might God's pruning help you get there?

4. WHAT OTHER BIBLE PEOPLE SHOW HOW GOD PRUNES US?

PROFILE #1:
Abraham, the man who gave his son to God.

[Read Genesis 22]

A key area in which God prunes us is relationships. Will we give God first place in our affections, ahead of even our closest family members (Luke 14:26)? Or will we let personal loyalties hinder what God wants to do through us?

Abraham faced just such a test. God had promised Abraham that through his son, Isaac, he would become a great nation (Genesis 12:1–3). But one day, when Isaac was still a child, God asked Abraham to give Isaac back.

> **"" TALK POINT ""**
>
> How do you think you would have responded if you had been in Abraham's shoes?

1. a. *What did God ask Abraham to do (Genesis 22:2)?* _____.

   b. *How quickly did Abraham respond (Genesis 22:3)?* _____.

2. *In Genesis 22:12, God reveals the purpose of the pruning: "Now I know that you* _____ *God, since you have not* _____ *your* _____, *your only son, from Me."*

3. *Has there ever been a time when God wanted you to serve Him in a given area but a key relationship left you unwilling to do it? What happened?*

4. *Of everyone who means the most to you personally, who would be your "Isaac"?*

> *Our heavenly Father never takes anything from his children unless he means to give them something better.*
>
> GEORGE MÜELLER

PROFILE #2:
Joseph, the man who gave his future to God.

[Read Genesis 37:1–11]

eXTRA Joseph had a promising start in life. He grew up as his father's favorite and showed many natural leadership talents. God told him through a dream that he would one day be a ruler. But first came years of slavery. Trace Joseph's eventful early life:

- ◆ Genesis 37:18–28—brutally sold into slavery.
- ◆ Genesis 39:19–20—unjustly imprisoned.
- ◆ Genesis 40:23—cruelly forgotten in jail.

1. *As with Abraham, God promised Joseph something, only to remove any apparent chance of it happening. Why might God have done this?*

2. *Read Genesis 39:21. Write down the three signs that God's pruning in Joseph's life was a sign of His favor:*

    a.

    b.

    c.

3. *When you look at the injustices Joseph suffered, you might conclude that he was in chastening. But his story shows that God was using negative circumstances to prepare a fruitful person for more fruit. Write down the invaluable lesson Joseph learned (see Genesis 50:18–20).*

" " TALK POINT " "

Can you think of a time when someone treated you unjustly or hurtfully?

Did you allow God to prune you through the experience, or do you think the experience was mostly wasted?

> *I owe more to the fire, and the hammer, and the file, than to anything else in my Lord's workshop.*
>
> **CHARLES SPURGEON**

5. HOW CAN I GET THE MOST OUT OF PRUNING?

Unlike the grape plant, a person can choose to either resist the Vinedresser or respond wholeheartedly. God wants you to know whether you are in pruning or discipline so that you can respond positively for your own good and for God's purposes for your life.

DISCIPLINE VERSUS PRUNING: A COMPARISON

Issue	Disciplining	Pruning
HOW DO YOU KNOW IT'S HAPPENING?	Pain	Discomfort
WHY IS IT HAPPENING?	You're doing something wrong (sin)	You're doing something right (bearing fruit)
WHAT IS YOUR LEVEL OF FRUITFULNESS?	No fruit	Fruit
WHAT IS THE VINEDRESSER'S DESIRE?	Fruit	More fruit
WHAT NEEDS TO GO?	Sin (disobeying the Lord)	Self (putting myself before God)
HOW SHOULD YOU FEEL?	Guilty, sad	Relief, trust
WHAT IS THE RIGHT RESPONSE?	Repentance (stop your sin)	Release (surrender to God)
WHEN DOES IT STOP?	When you stop your sin	When God is finished

1. *Do you find the descriptions above helpful? If so, what percentage of those in your church would you now say are in discipline? How many are in pruning?*

2. *If a Christian came to realize that he was being pruned when he thought he was being disciplined, how might it radically change his attitude?*

" " TALK POINT " "

Based on this chart, if a friend concluded that he was in pruning, what could you tell him that would really help?

6. RESPONDING FOR RESULTS

The apostle Paul understood the unseen but lasting results of pruning. His advice to all growing Christians who are confronted by the Vinedresser's shears could be summarized in three words: *rejoice, relinquish,* and *rest.*

1. <u>PHILIPPIANS 4:11-13</u>. *Instead of anxiety, I can* _____ *in His power and love.*

2. <u>PHILIPPIANS 4:4</u>. *Instead of complaining or criticizing, I can* _____
in His plan.
    a. *Have you been successful at this? Why do you think God asks it of us?*

    b. *Can you think of a time when you criticized the messenger of God's pruning rather than responding to God?*

3. <u>PHILIPPIANS 3:8</u>. *Instead of resisting, I can_____ this area to Him.*
    a. *The harder we hold onto what God wants us to let go of, the more pruning comes our way. So why do you think we so often resist letting go?*

    b. *What are some practical ways you might help yourself surrender something to God once and for all?*

DO I NEED TO APOLOGIZE TO GOD?

Many of us look back on our parents' discipline and realize that what seemed like unfair restriction or meddling was actually loving, wise direction. Often we feel the need to apologize to our parents for our negative responses.

Is there a similar unresolved offense in your relationship with God? Have you mistaken pruning for discipline? Has your negative response pushed you into a sinful response? If so, I encourage you to apologize to God. Tell Him you misunderstood His motives and His methods. Ask for His pardon. Then walk forward in the power of the truth and the freedom of forgiveness.

7. WHAT IS KEEPING ME FROM SURRENDERING TO GOD'S PRUNING?

KEY Unlike the grape plant, a person can choose to either resist the Vinedresser or respond wholeheartedly for a more productive life. But before the truth about fruitfulness can change you, you must identify your old thinking and see the error that is trapping you, then kick it out of your life!

If you recognize yourself in any of the false beliefs on this page, let God's Word prepare you to receive the work of abundance He wants for your life. Then write out your new breakthrough belief.

CUTTING LOOSE FROM PRUNING TANGLES

❏ *You may think,* "GOD IS PICKING ON ME UNFAIRLY." *But the truth is that God's pruning is proof of both His love and your potential.* 2 Corinthians 1:3–7; Hebrews 5:8–9; James 1:2–12; 1 Peter 1:6–7.

❏ *You assume,* "GOD HAS ABANDONED ME." *But the truth is that God is always with you, and right now He's intensively involved in your life.* Psalm 23; Psalm 139:1–6; Daniel 3:15–18; John 14:18; Romans 8:35–39.

❏ *You exclaim,* "GOD IS ASKING TOO MUCH!" *But the truth is that God is pruning you in the right way for the right length of time so you can receive what He wants to give.* Genesis 50:19–20; Job 23:8–10; 2 Corinthians 9:8.

❏ *You wonder,* "DOES GOD REALLY KNOW WHAT'S GOING ON?" *But the truth is that God is at work in your life according to a grand purpose that will bring abundant results.* Isaiah 55:8–9; Matthew 6:8, 25–34; Romans 11:33–36.

❏ *You reason,* "HOW COULD A LOVING GOD ALLOW THIS TO HAPPEN?" *But the truth is that because He is a loving God, He is faithfully committed to your ultimate good through every test.* Psalm 73; Romans 8:28, 37–39; 2 Corinthians 12:7–10.

My New Breakthrough Belief:

_____

_____

_____

My New Start in Surrendering to God

In the Uffizi Gallery in Florence, Italy, you can see what pruning looks like in marble.

Here's what I mean: Michelangelo, a famous sculptor of the Renaissance era, believed that his statues already existed inside the blocks of marble; his job was simply to remove all unnecessary marble until the hidden masterpiece was revealed. A series of unfinished pieces at the Uffizi reveals Michelangelo's creative process. Where the sculpting is complete, you see a perfectly smooth arm or torso. But where his chisel hasn't yet carved, you see only chunks of stone. As a result, the human figures appear caught inside the block of marble, trying to get out. No wonder the series is entitled *The Prisoners.*

Pruning is a lot like that. God is at work in your life and mine to reveal what only He can see in our future. He is the Master Sculptor. His goal is our beauty and freedom. As we close this study, I invite you to apply what you've learned:

If you had to identify one area in which, over the past year, the Lord seems to have been pruning you for abundance, where would it be? How should you respond?

Are you ready to respond in this area in such a way that God can work in your life for the benefits that only He can see right now? In the space below describe the conditions of your surrender to the Master's hand. Then sign and date your decision.

The conditions of my surrender

Signature   Date

My Prayer to Respond to God's Pruning

Dear God,
How often I've resisted Your work in my life,
seeing only the personal "loss" to me and not the permanent
gain for eternity. But now I see that all Your ways are kind
and loving and faithful. Forgive me for choosing my
priorities, my desires, and my ways over Yours.
How foolish and wasteful! You are the Master Vinedresser.
I surrender my whole life to You. Please accomplish
Your perfect plan for me. Prune me in the way and for
the time that You know to be best. Reshape me to be like
Your Son, Jesus, so that I can bring great pleasure to You,
and so that my life will bear great fruit for Your glory.
I praise You and thank You for Your love.
Amen.

I press on, that I may lay hold of that for which Christ Jesus has also
laid hold of me. Bretheren, I do not count myself to have apprehended;
but one thing I do, forgetting those things which are behind and reaching
forward to those things which are ahead, I press toward the goal
for the prize of the upward call of God in Christ Jesus.

PHILIPPIANS 3:12–14

Week Four

ABIDING

HOW GOD INVITES YOU
TO FLOURISH IN HIS PRESENCE

> "Abide in Me, and I in you. As the
> branch cannot bear fruit of itself,
> unless it abides in the vine, neither
> can you, unless you abide in Me.
> I am the vine, you are the branches.
> He who abides in Me, and I in him,
> bears much fruit, for without Me
> you can do nothing."
>
> JOHN 15:4–5

RECOMMENDED READING

Secrets of the Vine, Chapters 7–9
Secrets of the Vine Devotional, Week 4

GETTING STARTED

In week 1, we learned that there are four levels of fruitfulness—no fruit, fruit, more fruit, and much fruit. This week we look at what it takes to reach the highest level of abundance. But first...

Return with me to that scene in the lamplit circle. Jesus and His closest friends are walking toward the Garden of Gethsemane at night. They stop in an ancient vineyard. Can you sense the sadness of the moment? Humanly speaking, it's the beginning of the end. By the next afternoon, Jesus will be bleeding and battered, hanging from a cross....

Listen carefully to Jesus' good-bye. Because when you do, you'll hear Jesus pleading with His best friends *not* to leave Him. In fact, in just ten sentences, Jesus says "abide" or "remain" ten times.

And here is the truth we'll explore this week: Only in a flourishing, unbroken friendship with God can we reach the highest level of personal abundance *and* fulfillment. This is our final secret of fruitfulness.

THE THIRD SECRET OF THE VINE
If your life bears a lot of fruit, God will invite you to abide more deeply with Him, the result of which will be "much" fruit.

My friend, if you receive Jesus' words to you this week, if you genuinely encounter His sincere desire to be close to you, you'll never be the same. You will break through to a new spiritual experience of God as your Friend. And you'll begin to see a greater harvest of fruit for eternity than you ever thought possible.

THIS WEEK YOU'LL DISCOVER...

♦ why abiding leads to the highest level of fruitfulness.
♦ the biblical definition of the word *abiding*.
♦ examples of abiding from people in the Bible.
♦ common misconceptions that can keep you from abiding.
♦ how to break through to an ongoing, intimate relationship with God.

1. WHAT DO I BELIEVE ABOUT GETTING CLOSE TO GOD?

1. *Think of a time when you felt especially near to God. List three words that describe how that felt.*

MY "FRIENDSHIP WITH GOD" INVENTORY

2. *The following inventory will help you discover what you really believe about your potential for a closer and more rewarding friendship with God. Score your answers:*
   ❶ Strongly agree. ❷ Agree. ❸ Unsure. ❹ Slightly disagree. ❺ Strongly disagree.

___ I believe friendship with God requires little effort for Christians.

___ If I read my Bible and pray every day, intimacy with God happens automatically.

___ "Professional Christians"—pastors, missionaries, and choir members— have a huge advantage in getting closer to God.

___ A meaningful friendship with God isn't really possible since He's in heaven and I'm on earth.

___ It's God's move. If He wants to be close to me, it's up to Him to make Himself near and known.

___ YOUR SCORE: Add up your answers. If you scored...

21–25 CLOSE 'N' PERSONAL. *You cherish your friendship with God, and you want more of it.*

16–20 FREQUENTLY FRIENDLY. *You think a friendship with God is desirable, and you're in a good position to get closer.*

11–15 SOMEWHAT NEIGHBORLY. *You're not sure what to predict in a friendship with God, so you mind your manners.*

5–10 MOSTLY STRANGERS. *You don't think friendship with God is possible, so you apply your energies elsewhere.*

" " TALK POINT " "

Outside of your own family, who would you say is your closest friend?

What qualities about the relationship make it so meaningful and valuable to you?

2. WHAT DOES IT MEAN TO ABIDE?

KEY To abide means to remain intimately connected to Jesus Christ. In vineyard terms, abiding happens at the place where the branch connects to the vine. The greater our connection to Jesus, the more we tap into His power and presence—and the more fruit we can bear for Him.

In vineyard terms,

  abiding happens at the place

 where the branch

  connects to the vine.

Read 1 John 4:13–15. From this passage we see that we begin to abide when we accept Christ as our Savior. This kind of abiding is a supernatural gift from God. Yet in John 15:4 and 9, *abide* is used as an imperative—Jesus commanded His disciples to abide. That means that abiding for "much fruit" requires an action on our part.

1. *A word closely related to abiding is* fellowship. *According to 1 John 1:1–3 and 1 Corinthians 1:9, who can we have fellowship with?*

2. *Another synonym for abiding is* communion. *Second Corinthians 13:14 tells us that we can enjoy the communion of* _____.

3. Abide *can also be translated "remain" or "stay." What does this say about who is responsible when there is distance between you and God? How might knowing this change the way you approach intimacy with Him?*

> **" TALK POINT "**
>
> Have you gone through a period in your Christian life when you made little or no effort to be in close relationship to God, even though you knew you were His child? What did that feel like?

WELCOME TO THE PLACE OF ABIDING

In John 15, Jesus mentions three ways or "places" we abide:

1. <u>WE ABIDE IN CHRIST</u>. *Notice the wording of John 15:5. Jesus was describing a level of intimacy between Jesus and His friends that could continue even after His death. We don't remain with Jesus, or even near Jesus, but* _____ *Him—and He in us!*

GETTING TO KNOW HIM

The Son of God has come and has given us an understanding, that we may know Him who is true.

1 JOHN 5:20

Is the God of the universe knowable? Yes! In fact, coming to know God better is what abiding is all about. Paul was so convinced Christ was knowable that he wrote, "I also count all things loss for the excellence of the knowledge of Christ Jesus my Lord" (Philippians 3:8). And God told Jeremiah, "Let him who glories glory in this, that he understands and knows Me" (Jeremiah 9:24).

2. <u>WE ABIDE IN HIS LOVE</u>. *Read John 15:9–17.*
   a. *Jesus tells us that we are to abide in His* _____ *(v. 9), which is possible as we keep His* _____ *(v. 10).*
   b. *This passage echoes Jesus' teaching about the greatest commandment (Mark 12:28–34). How might abiding in God's love lead naturally to loving others?*

3. <u>WE ABIDE IN HIS WORD.</u> *In John 15:7, Jesus told His disciples to* _____ *in Christ and let His* _____ *abide in them. What are some practical ways to make this happen?*

" " TALK POINT " "

If Jesus were back on the earth, do you think He'd choose to build a friendship with you?

Would you seek out a friendship with Him?

3. WHY IS ABIDING SO IMPORTANT?

1. <u>ABIDING IS ONE OF GOD'S GREATEST DESIRES.</u> *From the Garden of Eden to the closing pages of Revelation, the Bible is a chronicle of God's initiatives to have a personal relationship with the human race.*

    a. *What does Revelation 3:20 reveal about God's desire for and active pursuit of friendship with us?*

    b. *How does this personal invitation make you feel? How often do you hear this knocking on the door to your heart? How do you tend to answer?*

2. <u>ABIDING IS ONE REASON GOD CREATED US.</u> *David expressed the longing of the human soul for God: "As the deer pants for the water brooks, so pants my soul for You, O God" (Psalm 42:1).*

    a. *Read Psalm 16:11 and 17:15. What do we find in God's presence?*

    b. *What are some ways people tend to look for personal fulfillment outside of intimacy with God? How successful are these efforts?*

    c. *On a scale of 1–10 (1 being low), how strong is your own desire to know God? Why do you think this is so?*

3. <u>ABIDING IS THE ONLY WAY WE CAN YIELD AN ABUNDANT HARVEST OF "MUCH FRUIT."</u> *Why do you think a deeper friendship with God and obedience to Him might result in more fruitfulness for eternity? (See John 15:5.)*

" " TALK POINT " "

If you were convinced that Jesus wants to abide with you even more than you do Him, what difference would this make in how you approach Him?

4. HOW DOES ABIDING LEAD TO "MUCH" FRUIT?

 KEY The branch that bears "much" fruit bears the highest yield possible. Surprisingly, the key to this abundance is not doing more *for* God, but being more *with* God. How does this work?

1. *Let's look more closely at what Jesus said in John 15:4–5:*

   > "AS THE BRANCH CANNOT BEAR FRUIT OF ITSELF, UNLESS IT ABIDES IN THE VINE, NEITHER CAN YOU, UNLESS YOU ABIDE IN ME. I AM THE VINE, YOU ARE THE BRANCHES. HE WHO ABIDES IN ME, AND I IN HIM, BEARS MUCH FRUIT; FOR WITHOUT ME YOU CAN DO NOTHING."

   a. *What activity on our part is the only source of real abundance?*

   b. *What startling truth does Jesus reveal about our ability to bear fruit at any level? What does this say to you about the importance of dependence upon God as we carry out good works?*

   c. *Read Matthew 11:28–30 and Galatians 6:9. How might abiding help us to not grow weary in doing God's work?*

2. *As we take more time to abide with God, we'll obviously have less time to do things for Him. That's why abiding for maximum fruitfulness requires a step of faith. You must believe that if you do less in order to abide more, God will increase your harvest to the highest levels possible. If you acted on this new belief today, what changes would you need to make in your life immediately?*

THE MIRACLE OF MORE FOR LESS

When you abide with God, He multiplies your efforts to bear fruit. The same things you did before to produce fruit will now yield much greater results—without more effort. Also notice the remarkable promise in John 15:7 related to abiding: "If you abide in Me, and My words abide in you, you will ask what you desire, and it shall be done for you." When we abide in Christ and His Word, our prayers change. His desires become our desires. And when we ask for them, God says yes.

5. WHO ELSE IN THE BIBLE CHOSE TO ABIDE?

PROFILE #1:
Mary and Martha, a tale of two sisters.

[Read Luke 10:38–42]

Mary, along with her sister Martha and brother Lazarus, lived near Jerusalem. Apparently, Jesus was a frequent guest. One day after He and the disciples had arrived, Martha scurried to meet needs while Mary sat at Jesus' feet. Martha asked Jesus to reprimand Mary, but Jesus gently rebuked Martha instead: "Martha, Martha, you are worried and troubled about many things. But one thing is needed, and Mary has chosen that good part, which will not be taken away from her" (vv. 41–42). This story illustrates several important principles of abiding:

1. ABIDING REQUIRES OUR TIME AND FOCUSED ATTENTION. *What are the "many things" that tend to distract you from spending time with God? What do you think Jesus meant by "one thing is needed"?*

2. ABIDING IS WITH A PERSON, NOT A PROGRAM OR BELIEF. *Jesus loved Mary and Martha (John 11:5). Notice Mary's desire to be near Jesus—do you experience the personal presence of the Lord during your quiet times? If it usually feels more like a program, what could you do to make your experience more personal in nature?*

3. ABIDING IS MEANT FOR EVERY BELIEVER, REGARDLESS OF AGE, TEMPERAMENT, OR LEVEL OF MATURITY. *Jesus wanted activity-minded Martha to choose abiding. What personal tendencies or circumstances do you need to realize might be keeping you from abiding?*

" " TALK POINT " "

Who do you identify with more in this story—Mary or Martha? Why?

4. <u>ABIDING IS AVAILABLE TO ALL BELIEVERS AT ANY TIME OR PLACE.</u>
   Jesus challenged Martha about her priorities, not her activities. Regular time set apart to wholly focus on God is where deep abiding begins. But we can abide with Him anywhere and at any time—while driving to work, folding laundry, or mowing the lawn. Brother Lawrence called this "practicing the presence of God."

   a. *Have you ever chosen to abide with Jesus while you were busy doing something else? Describe the experience.*

   b. *List three weekly activities that allow you to focus your mind and heart on fellowship with God.*

ANTICIPATION

*My soul waits for the Lord
more than those who watch for the morning.*

PSALM 130:6

PROFILE #2:
John, the disciple whom Jesus loved.
[Read 1 John 2:24–28; 4:7–16]

eXTRA It's not surprising that John was the disciple who recorded Jesus' teaching on abiding. Four times in his Gospel, John calls himself "the disciple whom Jesus loved." This was John's way of expressing his confidence in Jesus' affection for him personally. That this confidence was born of deep abiding is evidenced also in John's Epistles, where abiding is a favorite theme.

How would the value you place on abiding change if you felt as convinced as John that Jesus loves you personally?

6. HOW DO I GROW IN ABIDING?

1. PLAN A REGULAR TIME AND PLACE. *Most people find that mornings work best. Choose a place where you feel private and comfortable. Protect your daily appointment as if you were meeting with a king (which you are!). Write out Psalm 5:3 as a declaration of your intentions:*

2. PURPOSE TO SEEK GOD UNTIL YOU FIND HIM. *And you will find Him if you persevere because God will keep His promise: "Draw near to God and He will draw near to you" (James 4:8). Write out what David discovered about seeking God in Psalm 145:17–21:*

3. PRACTICE THE SPIRITUAL DISCIPLINES. *As used here, the word* discipline *is defined as a regular practice with an important and proven benefit. That's why you choose to do it even when you don't feel like it. Read the description of each spiritual discipline on the next page. Then rate how you're doing in this area at present (circle a number from 1=no activity to 5=extremely well) and describe one thing you can do to improve.*

ARE YOU PREOCCUPIED?

We are called to an everlasting preoccupation with God.

A. W. TOZER

SPIRITUAL DISCIPLINES

a. READ THE WORD OF GOD. *To abide, you read the Bible in order to meet its Author, and you receive His words as a letter to you.*
How I'm Doing: 1   2   3   4   5
One thing I could do to improve: _____

b. PRAY TO THE PERSON OF GOD. *To abide, you pursue an ongoing conversation with God. You practice honesty, immediacy, and careful listening.*
How I'm Doing: 1   2   3   4   5
One thing I could do to improve: _____

c. PRAISE AND WORSHIP GOD. *To abide, you respond to God appropriately—and He is worthy of your daily thanksgiving and adoration.*
How I'm Doing: 1   2   3   4   5
One thing I could do to improve: _____

d. WRITE TO GOD IN A SPIRITUAL JOURNAL. *To abide, you record what God is teaching you, remember His answers to your prayers, and trace His presence in your daily circumstances.*
How I'm Doing: 1   2   3   4   5
One thing I could do to improve: _____

e. FAST TO RECEIVE MORE OF GOD. *To abide, you set aside times to experience want (of food, for example) in order to allow God to fill you up with more of Himself.*
How I'm Doing: 1   2   3   4   5
One thing I could do to improve: _____

4. *What does your inventory show you about what you can expect from your relationship with God based on what you are investing in it?*

" " TALK POINT " "

Which of the disciplines do you feel would help you the most to abide more at this time in your life? How can you start that today?

7. WHAT CAN KEEP ME FROM ABIDING?

KEY If communion with God is such a deep desire of the human heart, why do so few Christians pursue it successfully? The culprit is often unrecognized attitudes or habits of thinking that cut us off from what we really want.

See if you recognize yourself in the "abiding busters" on this page (each example, while powerful, is wrong). Let the Bible help you discover a new breakthrough truth, and write it down (in your own words) in the space provided.

FIVE ABIDING BUSTERS

❑ THE "BUT I DON'T FEEL ANYTHING" FOUL-UP. *You assume if you didn't have strong emotions, nothing happened.* Psalm 145:18; 1 John 3:19–20.

❑ THE "HE DOESN'T LIKE ME" MUDDLE. *You believe God loves you, but you doubt that He actually likes you.* John 15:15; Ephesians 3:17–19; 1 John 3:1.

❑ THE "I'M TOO BUSY" BLUNDER. *You let your schedule keep you from regular abiding, but you think God will connect with you anyway.* Isaiah 40:31; Matthew 6:33; Matthew 11:28.

❑ THE "SIN DOESN'T MATTER" MISTAKE. *You think ongoing disobedience won't keep you from abiding, especially if you experience pleasant feelings during church.* Psalm 15; Psalm 66:18–20; James 4:8; 1 John 1:5–7.

❑ THE "GOING THROUGH THE MOTIONS" NOTION. *You think Bible reading and prayer are proof you're having a relationship with God.* 1 Samuel 16:7; Psalm 27:4–8; Matthew 5:6.

My New Breakthrough Belief:

_____

_____

_____

_____

My New Start in Abiding

Suppose you're on your third week of setting aside time to abide with God. Things could hardly be going worse. You've missed a string of morning appointments. Last night you got into a shouting match with your teenager. This morning you slept late. Feeling cranky and without brushing your teeth, you stumble into your study to grab your Bible when...

You notice a shining angel seated in your chair. Shocked and trembling, you gasp, "Wha...what are you doing here?"

"I'm supposed to meet God here right now," the angels says calmly. "I have an appointment."

"But...so do I," you reply.

This story leads to my question: *Assuming God could keep only one appointment this morning, whom would He choose—you or the angel?* Explain your answer.

My friend, there's no contest. God would choose time with you in a heartbeat.

Will you keep your appointment? You see, in abiding, it's always our move. To abide, we simply must accept the astounding offer of a daily, life-changing friendship with God—and act on it.

As we close this study on fruitfulness, I invite you to choose to pursue the friendship of a lifetime and a harvest for eternity. If you're ready, write down what you will do to begin meeting with God, and write down the time and place of your next appointment.

My commitment to abide with God

Signature   Date

My Prayer to Abide

Dear Lord,
I draw near to You today—oh, please draw near to me!
Thank You that You have promised to do this.
Nothing matters more in my life than You—Your presence,
Your favor, Your friendship. Yet I confess that I
so often pursue lesser priorities and forget to abide in You.
I have often offended You, disrespected Your wishes,
and thoughtlessly injured our relationship.
Please forgive me, Lord. I promise to seek You
with all my heart. Reveal Yourself to me in new ways
even today. May Your abiding presence in my life
result in such fruitfulness for You that heaven will
celebrate the results—today and for all eternity.
Amen.

> We...do not cease to pray for you, and to ask that you may be filled with
> the knowledge of His will in all wisdom and spiritual understanding;
> that you may walk worthy of the Lord, fully pleasing Him, being fruitful
> in every good work and increasing in the knowledge of God.
>
> COLOSSIANS 1:9–10

A LIFE GOD REWARDS™

The BreakThrough Series, Book Three

In this soul-stirring follow-up to his runaway bestsellers *The Prayer of Jabez* and *Secrets of the Vine*, Bruce Wilkinson leads you to some astonishing and entirely biblical answers about why what you do today matters forever. He gives a fresh view of the eternal existence you're investing in right now—showing why it's worth it (at a thousand percent return on investment) to serve God with all your heart for all your life!

ISBN 1-57673-967-7

www.prayerofjabez.com
www.jabezmillion.com

What Happened to Your Dream?

ISBN 1-59052-201-X

Taking up where *The Prayer of Jabez* left off, Bruce Wilkinson shows how to identify and overcome the obstacles that keep millions from living the life they were created for. Readers will understand that they were made for a purpose—and their life dream is a gift from God to guide them to their destiny. Sharing practical, biblical keys to fulfilling a dream, the bestselling author reveals that there's no limit to what God can accomplish when we choose to cherish the dreams He gives us and pursue them for His honor.

Also available

Printed in the United States
by Baker & Taylor Publisher Services